# Caring For Loved Ones At Home

An illustrated, easy-to-follow guide to short and long-term care

## 6th Anniversary Edition

## Harry van Bommel

Resources Supporting Family
and Community Legacies Inc.

Scarborough, Ontario 2002

Cover and illustrations by Diane Huson, Whitby, Ontario.

Author's cover photograph by John Telian of *Telian Photo Studio*, Scarborough, Ontario.

**National Library of Canada Cataloguing in Publication**
van Bommel, Harry
    Caring for loved ones at home/Harry van Bommel. 6th anniversary ed.
Illustrations by Diane Huson.

Includes bibliographical references and index.
ISBN 1-55307-006-2
    1. Home nursing. I. Resources Supporting Family and Community Legacies Inc. II. Title.

R726.8V3 2002          649'.8          C2002-901663-0


To contact the author, write or call:

Resources Supporting Family and Community Legacies Inc.

11 Miniot Circle, Scarborough, Ontario  CANADA  M1K 2K1

(416) 264-4665, E-mail: harry@legacies.ca

Printed and bound in Canada by Webcom Limited.

**Remember to talk to a professional health care provider (e.g., nurse, doctor, physiotherapist or pharmacist) before trying any of the tips and techniques in this book to make sure you are doing them correctly.**

In memory of **Moeder**, **Vader** and **Opa**, with love and gratitude.


In memory of **Brychan (Taffy) Jones Price** who allowed others to show him the same love, acceptance and care he gave so freely to them.


In honor of **Rieky Haas; Philo van Enckevort; Annie and Leo van Ryswyk** and **their extended families** who all model caring for loved ones with such joyful compassion.


Dedicated to **Janet**, **Bram** and **Joanna** who lovingly share in this continuing adventure.

# Table of Contents

# Foreword

On behalf of the Saint Elizabeth Health Care Foundation, and together with the organization from which you received this book, I am pleased to offer *Caring for Loved Ones at Home* to Canadian families free of charge. The Foundation is very proud to be sponsoring the sixth anniversary edition printing of this charitable publication which is intended to help family members and friends more effectively manage the home care needs of their loved ones.

This very important initiative was embraced by the Saint Elizabeth Health Care Foundation for a second time because of an ever present need to provide instruction and information to people who are caring for loved ones at home. The Foundation's charitable contribution to publish, print and distribute the previous edition of *Caring for Loved Ones at Home* together with the charitable home care book *Family Hospice Care*, made the largest dissemination of palliative care information possible in the history of Canada, for which the Foundation was named *Outstanding Philanthropist of the Year* by the Ontario Palliative Care Association.

The Saint Elizabeth Health Care Foundation was established in 1997 to raise awareness and charitable funding to enhance and expand the health care services offered in the home and community.

As such, this copy of *Caring for Loved Ones at Home* was made available to you as a result of charitable support. If you would like to help make this book available, free of charge, to more Canadian families, please consider making a tax-deductible charitable donation to the Saint Elizabeth Health Care Foundation by mail at the address listed below or by telephone using the toll-free number provided. Also, we would very much like to hear from you – let us know if this book met your needs or if you have suggestions for improvements. We have included a brief evaluation form at the back of this book – your comments will help keep this publication up-to-date!

In closing, I would like to thank Harry van Bommel for presenting the Saint Elizabeth Health Care Foundation with the opportunity to partner, once again, in this invaluable project and for his time, research and expertise in the development of this book.

Sister Roberta Freeman, C.S.J.
Secretary
Saint Elizabeth Health Care Foundation
June, 2002
90 Allstate Parkway, Suite 300
Markham, Ontario L3R 6H3
Telephone: 1 (800) 463-1763

# Acknowledging The Sponsors

We would like to thank the following individuals and sponsors for making this book available to you, free of charge.

Saint Elizabeth Health Care Foundation sponsored the first free printing and distribution of over 75,000 copies of this book with copies in more than 380 home and hospice care organizations across Canada. Their ongoing sponsorship of this second free distribution is a testament to their commitment to helping family, friends and neighbors provide basic, practical and comforting care for loved ones at home. I am grateful to the following individuals and health care organizations for contributing funds for this book:

*100 Mile District Hospice Palliative Care Society*, BC
*Abbotsford Hospice Society*, Abbotsford, BC
*Algoma VON*, Sault Ste. Marie, ON
*Annapolis Valley VON*, Kentville, NS
*Baryshore Health Care*, Cornwall, ON
*The Bernard Betel Centre for Creative Living*, Toronto, ON
*Brockville Leeds & Grenville VON*, Brockville, ON
*Bruce Peninsula Hospice*, Wiarton, ON
*Canadian Cancer Society, Cancer Information Service*, Regina, SK
*Cariboo Memorial Hospital*, Williams Lake, BC
*Chatham VON Geranium House*, Chatham, ON
*Chilliwack Hospice Society*, Chilliwack, BC
*Chilliwack Palliative Care Program*, Chilliwack, BC
*Dr. David A. Coleman*, Corner Brook, NF
*Cowichan Valley Hospice Society*, Duncan, BC
*Council on Palliative Care*, McGill, Montreal, PQ
*Crossroads Hospice Society*, Port Moody, BC
*Delta Hospice Society*, Delta, BC
*Dundas County Hospice*, Williamsburg, ON
*Emmanuel House*, Hamilton, ON
*Family Caregiver Centre*, Calgary, AB
*Grey Bruce Health Services*, Owen Sound, ON

*Haldimand-Norfolk CCAC*, Simcoe, ON
*Health and Community Services*, St. John's, NF
*Hospice & Palliative Care Manitoba*, Winnipeg, MB
*Hospice Association of Ontario LifeLine*, Toronto, ON
*Hospice Huntsville*, Huntsville, ON
*Hospice Muskoka*, Bracebridge, ON
*Hospice of Peel*, Mississauga, ON
*Hospice of Providence*, Brockville, ON
*Hospice Quinte*, Belleville, ON
*Hospice Peterborough*, Peterborough, ON
*Hospice Wellington*, Guelph, ON
*The Huson Family*, Whitby, ON
*Interlink Community Cancer Nurses*, Toronto, ON
*Kootenay Boundary Community Health*, Castlegar, BC
*Suzanne Leece*, Brantford, ON
*Lunenburg & Queens Counties Palliative Care*, Bridgewater, NS
*Medicine Hat Palliative Care Society*, Medicine Hat, AB
*Mid-Island Hospice Society*, Nanaimo, BC
*Mid-Valley Palliative Care*, Laltare, NS
*Nelson and District Hospice Society*, Nelson, BC
*Newfoundland Cancer Treatment & Research Foundation*, St. John's, NF
*Niagara-on-the-Lake Community Palliative Care*, ON
*Nightingdale Nursing*, Saskatoon, SK
*NOR-MAN R.H.A.*, The Pas, MB
*North Durham Hospice*, Uxbridge, ON
*The North of Smokey Palliative Care/Hospice Society*, Neils Harbour, NS
*North Perth Community Hospice*, Listowel, ON
*Northwood Homecare Ltd*, Halifax, NS
*ONS Ontario Nursing Services Limited*, Markham, ON
*Palliative Pain & Symptom Management*, Peterborough, ON
*Para Med Health Services Ottawa*, ON
*Parkland Regional Health Authority*, Dauphin, MB
*Peace Palliative Care Society*, Peace River, AB

*Penticton and District Hospice Society*, Penticton, BC
*Pineland Home Care*, Prince Albert, SK
*Queen Elizabeth II HSC*, Palliative Care Program, Halifax, NS
*Quinte Healthcare Corporation*, Belleville, ON
*Renfrew County CCAC*, Pembroke, ON
*RHA Central Manitoba Inc.*, Portage la Prairie, MB
*Ridge Meadows Hospice Society*, Maple Ridge, BC
*St. Joseph's Health Care*, London, ON
*Ste Anne VON*, Beaconsfield, PQ
*Ste Rose General Hospital*, Ste Rose, MB
*Salvation Army Sylvia House Hospice*, Kanata, ON
*Sarnia-Lambton VON*, Sarnia, ON
*Simcoe County Pain and Symptom Management Program*, Barrie, ON
*Souris Valley Regional Care Centre*, Weyburn, SK
*South East Health Care Corporation*, Moncton, NB
*South Eastman Health Authority*, St. Pierre, MB
*South Okanagan General Hospital*, Oliver, BC
*South Westman Regional Health Authority Inc.*, Deloraine, MB
*Southampton Palliative Care Team*, Southampton, ON
*Sylvia Home Hospice, Salvation Army*, Kanata, ON
*Heather Taylor*, Pasadena, NF
*Thunder Bay CCAC/Pain and Symptom Management*, ON
*Trinity Home Hospice*, Toronto, ON
*Upper Skeena Hospice*, Hazelton, BC
*Valley Regional Hospital*, Kentville, NS
*White Rock/South Surrey Hospice Palliative Care*, White Rock, BC


**DISCLAIMER**: The views expressed in this book are those of the author and not necessarily those of any of the sponsors.

# Acknowledgements

I am grateful to the following people for their editorial advice: **Cathryn Allen**, Program Manager of the Palliative Care Program, Camp Hill Medical Center, Halifax, Nova Scotia; **Gloria Repetto** and **Florence Bell**, Head Nurse and Nursing Supervisor respectfully at Victoria General Hospital, Halifax; **Members of the Canadian Home Care Association**; **Dr. Ina Cummings**, Medical Director for Palliative Care at Camp Hill Medical Center; **Shari Douglas**, Home Care Case Manager in Owen Sound, Ontario; **Diane Huson**, illustrator, Whitby, Ontario; **Connie Smith**, Long-Term Care Co-Ordinator for Kincardine and District General Hospital, Ontario; **Deb Thivierge**, Human Services Consultant and partner in Paradigm Partners, Toronto, Ontario; **Glenna Thornhill**, Home Care Nurse, Camp Hill Medical Center; and **Dorothy Woodward**, retired home support worker, Parksville, British Columbia.

This revised edition was enhanced by the suggestions made by **Nadia Hladin**, Physiotherapist and Client Services Manager for the Community Care Access Centre of Peel; **Blair Henry** and **June Galbraith** of Trinity Home Hospice in Toronto, **Kit Martin**, RN, of the Palliative Care Services of York Region, and **Robert Ting, MD, FRCP(C)** a Nephrologist practicing in Toronto. Each of these professionals provided freely of their time and resources to help make home care a more positive experience for us all.

I am grateful to **Beverley Powell-Vinden** of PowerPhrase Communications in Mississauga, Ontario for making this book more readable.

My sincerest thanks and love to Janet Klees who helped provide home care to my father and who edits all of my work. She is my inspiration along with our children Bram and Joanna.

# Introduction

This book is meant to help people who need extra health care support at home. It does not matter if the person is recovering from an illness or surgery or whether they have a more chronic condition. The tips in this book will help both that person and their family members and friends who are providing support. **Talk to a professional health care provider (e.g., nurse, doctor, physiotherapist or pharmacist) before trying any of these tips and techniques to make sure you are doing them correctly. You want to make sure that you do not hurt your loved one or yourself as you provide care.**

The simple line drawings are meant to illustrate specific points in the instructions. Use them as guides to help you practice each of the different techniques. Remember that you are not trying to be a professional nurse. Instead you are trying to help someone you care about. These techniques will help you do exactly that. Be proud of your accomplishments. You are making a real difference in someone's life. Without you, they might not be able to stay in the comfort of their own home. When you are trying a new technique, don't be shy to ask the person you are helping to tell you what is working and what you might try to do differently. You are not doing this alone. You are working together with the person you are caring for so that both of you feel satisfied with the results.

Wherever you live, there is probably some form of Home Care Program available through your health care system. Find out at the hospital, through your family doctor, or through your telephone directory about services that are available in your area. Through such a program you will meet your home care case manager who can be an invaluable resource to get you the support you need to stay at home.

I helped both of my parents and grandfather to live at home until they died. I have also helped other loved ones who were ill, recovering from an illness or getting their strength back after giving birth. During the first few times I was reminded of how little I knew about caring for someone at home. With practice, I was learning more each time I helped someone at home or even in the hospital. I hope you find this book will spare you some of the 'trial and error' learning I went through. The information may also help you to ask the kinds of questions to get the support you and your loved ones need.

We must always remember that everyone in our lives has gifts to offer. It does not matter whether they are young or old, women or men, family members or friends or if they are disabled in some way. They can all participate, in varying degrees, in providing home care. Do not be shy in asking for specific help with errands, cooking, cleaning or providing physical or emotional support. Encourage their efforts. Ask for help when you need it.

**Note**: This is a short book. Therefore, we cannot cover every kind of health care situation you, or a loved one, may experience. *Adapt the information in this book to meet your needs. If you cannot find what you need in this book, ask your home care case manager, visiting home nurse, family doctor, pharmacist, social worker, librarian, or bookstore employee for more specific information.*

Sincere Best Wishes

HARRY VAN BOMMEL, Scarborough, Ontario

# What To Do In An Emergency

Talk to your doctor and health care team about who should be called for what type of emergency. Keep a list of their names and telephone numbers by the telephone and in your pocket. What may feel like an emergency may only need some telephone help from your doctor, nurse, social worker or home care case manager.

In almost all other emergency situations where you cannot deal with whatever is happening, call 911 or your local hospital, fire department or ambulance service. **Do not** call 911 if someone has died a natural, expected death at home, except in Quebec where legal procedures are in place to prevent resuscitation efforts on behalf of emergency staff. Instead, call your family doctor who can tell you what you should do next.

If you are expecting to care for someone at home, and have enough time to plan for that situation (e.g., someone is having surgery in 6 months) take an emergency first aid course or upgrading program. There are also family health care programs offered through local organizations including St. John Ambulance, The Red Cross, community colleges and others. The more you know about what to do in an emergency situation, the more comfortable you will feel and the more control you will have during the situation.

As with all good planning, you should think about what you will do in different situations **before** they happen. Just as we should plan our fire escape route from our home, we should also know what to do if someone gets seriously ill at home. The more we think about these situations in advance, the more we will act naturally and with relative calm if the situation ever happens.

# Home Care Examples

The following are some stories of how different people met their home care needs. For Jennifer, all of her home care was provided by family, friends and familiar health care providers. Francis needed a mix of family and special home care programs offered through the health care system. Jorge has to rely, almost exclusively, on the professional services offered through Home Care Programs and other community organizations. Justin's story highlights some of the similarities and differences of providing care to children at home. Sara's daughter Julie lives thousands of miles away yet is actively involved in the home care of her mother. These stories give us examples of what we might do in similar circumstances.

## Home Birth

Jennifer has decided to have a home birth if her pregnancy continues to go well. Her husband Joe is a little nervous but agrees as long as the midwives teach him what to do if there is an emergency in the middle of the night. As Jennifer's pregnancy continues, there are some typical ups and downs and concerns. All of these are met with compassion and honest communication between Jennifer, Joe, their midwives and their family doctor.

When the baby announces it is time to arrive, Jennifer and Joe call their midwives and their two friends, Susan and Margaret, and prepare their bedroom for the birth. Jennifer has time for a hot shower while Joe gets their young son, Daniel ready for a day with his 'Auntie' Margaret. When Margaret arrives, she takes Daniel out for a morning full of pre-planned activities. When Susan arrives, she begins to make some muffins for everyone and prepares tea and other 'comfort foods' for Jennifer, Joe and the midwives. When the midwives arrive, they have all the equipment one would find in a community hospital for deliveries, and they equip the room using towels to cover the equipment that will likely not be needed. They come in and out of the room to check on Jennifer, but for the most part, leave Jennifer and Joe together.

When the baby is ready to come out, Joe helps support Jennifer while the midwives talk Jennifer through the process. It takes different body positions, careful attention to breathing and Jennifer's loving attention to her baby. With the midwives gentle assistance, the baby is born at 12:12 p.m. just in time for Daniel to see his new sister. The midwives help clean up the room and one stays during the afternoon to make sure that everything is going well. Joe, other family members, friends and the midwives continue to provide home care support to Jennifer and the new baby for the next few days and weeks until everyone is strong again. Joe helps Jennifer wash herself in bed. He also helps her begin to move around the house and go to the washroom. Jennifer, Joe and Daniel are all proud of Maria's arrival in the safety and comfort of their own home.

## Recovering at Home

Francis lives on a farm about 25 miles from the nearest hospital. One night she wakes up in extreme pain. Her husband Willy rushes her to hospital where she undergoes emergency surgery. After about a week in the hospital, Francis is able to go home to recover. Willy has to spend most of the time out in the fields as this is harvest time. However, he always gets back to prepare Francis a good lunch and supper before going out to work a little longer.

Their daughter Marion, still lives at home and is able to help around the house when she is not at work. Marion makes sure that Francis takes the right medication at the right times, helps her mother do some simple washing up in bed, and helps her to the washroom. She cleans the linen on the bed regularly so that Francis is comfortable. Marion tries to be home when the nurse arrives so she and her mother can ask the nurse specific questions and record the nurse's answers. She cooks and freezes some meals so that her father only has to warm them up the next day.

Every day during the first week at home, a visiting nurse comes to change Francis' dressing. The surgery was major, so Francis cannot have a bath and the visiting nurse gives her a sponge bath in bed. After the first week, the nurse only comes every third day for another two weeks. By then Francis is able to take care of her own personal care and will be back to full strength in another three weeks.

## Long-Term Care at Home

Jorge is 82 years old and lives in a Home for the Aged in a big city. His wife died 11 years ago and he has no family living nearby. He has difficulty getting around so he uses a motorized scooter. His Home Care Case Manager arranged for him to get his bed raised so that it is easier to get in and out of it alone at night. She also arranged to have Jorge's bathtub adapted with strong holding bars to make it easier to use. An adaptive toilet seat is also used so that Jorge does not have to bend as far to sit down.

A nurse comes every three days to help him shower and wash his hair. A homemaker comes once a week to give his singe-room apartment a good cleaning and do some of his laundry. The homemaker also prepares a nutritious lunch and supper for him. Some of Jorge's other meals come through the community group Meals on Wheels and the rest he cooks himself or eats with friends in his building.

A volunteer comes to visit Jorge for a few hours every week. Jorge and David chat about common interests, play some cribbage and make plans for special occasions like the winter holidays, shopping trips, drives in the country or a simple stroll around the building. David understands some basic home care skills so he is able to help Jorge go to the washroom, help review the charts left by the visiting nurses or give him a wonderful massage just before leaving for the night. They have become friends over the past few years and David invites Jorge to his home once every month or two to share in some family activities.

Jorge had to go to hospital suddenly with a heart problem. Before he returned home, an occupational therapist visited his apartment to see if there was other equipment that could be brought in to help Jorge with his daily tasks. Home Care arranged to bring in a few more metal bars that Jorge could hold onto in his kitchenette and by his bed. They also recommended that Jorge subscribe to an emergency telephone signal that he would wear around his neck. If he fell or could not get to a phone, he just presses the button and a signal goes to a business that calls a neighbor to check on him.

Jorge is able to stay in his home because of the services available in his community. If he becomes less able to care for himself, however, he will require further services not yet available to him in his own home. Since he has no family or close friends nearby to help, he will need to go into a long-term care facility or nursing home. This frightens Jorge but he continues to hope that it will never come to that for him, as it has for so many of his friends who used to live in the same building.

## Caring for a Child

Many of the suggestions in this book hold true for children as well. A few extra points are illustrated by Justin's story.

Justin is 7 years old and was in the hospital for surgery on his elbow, which he injured in a soccer game. His parents, Doreen and Tyrone, had talked with his physician about what would happen, the after-care situations that might come up and what services were available at the hospital and for home care for both Justin and his family.

They answered all of Justin's questions honestly and in simple terms. They also gave him information that he didn't know to ask for that would give him some comfort and relieve some of his natural anxiety. They never overwhelmed him with long answers but broke down the questions into manageable chunks. They'd ask him to repeat, in his words, some of the explanations to make sure he understood what they were saying. Before the surgery and after, they used library books about hospitals, surgery and recovery to help him understand he was alone in having certain feelings and fears.

Whether in the hospital or at home, Doreen and Tyrone never gave Justin a promise they couldn't keep. They told him what to expect, how long it would probably take and if it would hurt. They didn't want him surprised or frustrated.

When Justin cried in fear, anger, pain or frustration, his parents comforted him and helped him get through. They used distractions (e.g., music, television, books, stories, laughter and games) to speed along the long waits during appointments and his recovery. They brought in friends and family to provide company and further distractions. To help

Justin cope with any discomfort or for particularly anxious moments, they used techniques like visualizations (having Justin close his eyes and take him on a peaceful adventure he could imagine in his mind), deep breathing, or squeezing a hand.

Children and adults feel a loss of control when they are sick or recovering. By letting Justin choose which arm a nurse would use to get a blood sample, or what foods he could eat or which friends to invite over, Doreen and Tyrone gave Justin choices and a sense of control during a difficult time.

## Long Distance Care

Julie's mother, Sara, lives a thousand miles away in her hometown. Julie is worried that her mother, now in her early 80s, will not be well cared for if her physical or mental abilities diminish. There are no siblings living near by and Sara relies on Julie's semi-annual visits to help her arrange medical, legal and financial affairs.

Rather than wait for an emergency to happen, Julie has done the following:

She has spent the past several years talking with her mother's friends and neighbors to create a support circle [similar to what is described later in this book]. A next door neighbor of many years has agreed to check in on Sara each day to make sure she is okay. If a problem arises, the neighbor will call one of several members of the support circle who has agreed to look after medical, legal or financial matters. If Sara needs some extra physical support at home, the circle has agreed to co-ordinate care with the local home care program and family physician with regular telephone direction from Julie. The circle members have also agreed to make regular visits during times of need so that no single member of the circle has to feel overwhelmed with Sara's care.

Julie has also made visits with Sara to her family doctor, local bank, and lawyer to make necessary arrangements and pass along Julie's telephone number in case of emergency. Sara has made Julie her power of attorney for health care. At present, Sara is able to maintain control over her own legal and financial matters.

In a more recent visit, Julie has gone over legal, funeral and financial matters so that in case of emergency, she knows where Sara's investments are kept, her Social Insurance Number, health numbers, insurance policies, will, credit cards, what funeral plans have been made, etc. Julie knows where all the important documents are kept including birth certificate, marriage certificate, and veteran's papers for her father, etc. She has also copied a directory of important telephone numbers so that she can be in immediate contact with the people who can best help Sara at any given time.

Sara has made copies of her home, car, and safety deposit keys. When the two visit together, they go over these matters but spend more time on sharing memories, visiting friends and nurturing their relationship.

"It isn't easy living so far away. We are doing the best we can but it is scary for both of us. I call almost everyday for a quick 'catch-up'. I searched for the best long-distance telephone rate I could get. We send each other 'care' packages with little gifts to remind each other of how important we are in each other's life. We don't have a perfect relationship, of course. There are days when we don't talk to each other because of a disagreement. She sometimes thinks I am trying to take over her life and I sometimes think she isn't doing enough to take care of herself and be safe. I worry that she might die alone in her home and she worries about dying alone in a hospital or nursing home. There is so much to work out but we are trying and we don't give up on each other."

These stories illustrate just some of the situations that might arise where someone requires extra support at home. Other situations may include parents caring for a child with disabilities, adult children caring for an ailing parent at home, a partner caring for a loved one with cancer or AIDS, or a family caring for someone who wants to live at home until they die.

Whatever the circumstances, providing care for a loved one at home involves some of the basic skills described in this book. If possible, it helps to do some of the caregiving for someone in hospital where the nurses and other professionals can teach you specific techniques. It makes caring for someone at home a lot easier if you have had the chance to practice under the supervision of skilled caregivers.

# Understanding How Illness Affects You And Your Family

Whenever I ask people if they would like to be a patient -- they all answer no! No one likes to be sick. Few of us enjoy having others take care of us except to be spoiled for a few days when we have the flu.

Long-term care can be quite frustrating for people and for those who care for them. Most of us would prefer to give the care rather than receive it. We have been brought up in the last 50 years to believe that allowing people to care for you is a burden to them. For those of us who have cared for others for quite some time, we recognize that often it is an honor and a pleasure to care for someone we love. There are times of great love, intimacy and laughter. There are also times of frustration and exhaustion. Often the difficulties do not come from taking care of someone else but because we forget to take care of ourselves or we do not ask for enough support from family, friends and community services. Some of the frustration comes from trying to understand and benefit from the complex health care system where we live.

The people who spend most of their time caring for someone they love need physical, emotional, spiritual and information supports just like the person who is getting home care. We often do not know how to ask for these supports and many people do not know how to offer them -- so the needed support is not there. One of the last sections of this book, *Creating Your Own Support Team*, is one way to change that. Modify the list of suggestions to meet your own needs. ***People generally love to help if they know it is only for a few hours every week or two. They will cut lawns, get groceries, walk your dog, pick up people at the airport,***

*or prepare a frozen meal you can use whenever you want.*
You only have to give people an excuse to help and most are
more than happy to do it. They want a specific task or duty to
perform to show they care and respect the person who is
getting home care.

There are a few other things you can do to make home
care more successful:

• Understand that your lives have changed for a while and
that you cannot do everything you used to, or when you used
to do it. Recognize as well (and this is just as important) that
you will be doing new things that will enrich your life, make a
real difference in the life of your loved one and will help you
remember what is truly important in life. This is a time of
both giving and receiving. This is also a time that will make
you stronger if you get the supports and information you
need.

• Understand that both the person who is receiving care at
home and those giving the care must work to help each other.
In other words, if your mother is at home sick and the rest of
the family is helping, you must all share in supporting each
other. Your mother must recognize that she is still your
mother and has gifts to offer you even though she is sick. She
still needs to be treated as a mother rather than a sick person.
She still needs to offer her motherly advice and wisdom. She
can still participate in her own care, to her best ability, while
also doing things to provide support to her family. As much
as she can, she should continue to offer her gifts of favorite
recipes, her needlework or letter writing, or her enjoyment of
singing or playing an instrument.

• She must not expect service that one gets from servants just as you cannot expect to provide that kind of service most of the time. While she is being the most helpful person she can be, you need to recognize that you would not want to change places with her and that she is going through a difficult time. Working together and communicating honestly will provide each of you the support you need. If you do not have that kind of relationship, you may need some help to improve the relationship you have. No one is a servant and no one is the master. You are all in this situation together doing the best you can with the knowledge and skills you have right now.

• You will need to plan ahead to meet the changes in your lives. If you feel overwhelmed with everything that is happening, ask for help from your home care co-coordinator, family doctor, or friends. Ask them to help you schedule your activities differently so that there is time to rest, relax and think rather than rush all the time. Other people have done this too and we can all learn from their experiences. Perhaps there are self-help support groups in your area to provide extra information and encouragement.

• Both the person who is ill and their family members may need more knowledge and skills to give the necessary support to each other. Learn as much as you can from this book and others listed in the references. The best people to learn from are the visiting home nurses so stay in the room with them as they nurse your loved one. Ask questions and offer to help so that you can practice the skills you need.

• Try to keep as many of your typical contacts as you can. Neither the person nor the family members should isolate themselves completely from those who love them. Your other family, friends and neighbors can provide you with the kind of emotional and spiritual support we all need. Again, they may not know how to offer, so ask them over for tea or take some time away from home to meet them somewhere else for a little break. If you do not know anyone who will stay with your loved one at home while you go out, ask your home care coordinator, visiting home nurse or family doctor for some volunteer services in your community that may be able to help. There are also some organizations that provide what is called 'respite care' to family members to give them some free time. Ideally the person who is ill should not have to leave home to give their family members a rest. It is better if the family is given an opportunity to have a weekend away or some similar time off.

• Understand that people's personalities do not change very much because of illness. If someone was very happy and family-oriented before their illness, they will probably remain that way now. If someone was quite unhappy and grouchy before, they will not suddenly become happy and enjoy everyone's company. This is just as true for family members caring for someone. The more we understand this basic truth, the less frustration we will have when people do not suddenly change to suit our needs. When there are significant changes in personality one should check about possible side effects from medication or a physical cause (e.g., dementia, brain cancer).

• Each of us deals with stress differently. This is just as true with the stress of an illness or some of the stress of caring for someone else. The more you recognize how someone has dealt with stress in the past the more you can help them deal positively with this stress. Whatever people have done in the past, they will probably do again. Listening to them and helping them to sort out other possible ways of dealing with stress will help you both.

• Few people enjoy hearing about how someone else has had the "exact same illness or condition and you should have seen how bad they had it!" These kinds of comparisons are not very helpful. If you have ever had your wisdom teeth removed or have been pregnant you will instantly know what we mean. Avoid comparing people's conditions and how well they are dealing with it compared to other people's experiences.

• When you have time away from caregiving or receiving care, you may want to join others to find ways to support those in the community who have long-term care commitments. You may also begin to discuss with community leaders, employers and politicians how we can adapt our systems to provide the economic stability and personal support that people need who are caring for others full time in their home. This group of mostly women is saving our country billions of dollars in institutional care but we often isolate them, force them to quit jobs they enjoy and provide them with little physical, emotional, spiritual and information support to care for loved ones at home. You only have to imagine what it is like to care for someone with dementia at home, or someone with physical disabilities requiring round-the-clock care, to understand how important it is that we all support each other in caring for loved ones at home. What we do for maternity leave we should do for people providing short and longer-term home care.

From personal experience I know that home care has many positive moments and some frustrating and angry ones. This is typical. You have all had jobs, relationships and vacations that included positive and negative experiences. That is reality for most of us. Home care is no different.

**The greatest predictor of how much you get out of this time together is whether or not you believe home care is a wonderful opportunity for everyone to slow down their lives and share in a common, life-defining experience.** If you believe that, you will be fine.

When you experience difficulties, talk to your home care coordinator, visiting home nurse, family doctor and other family members and friends to get their help.

# Adapting Your Home And Getting The Right Equipment

When someone at home needs some extra health care it may be helpful to adapt your home in some of the following ways.

Perhaps the person will need to stay in bed or is unable to move around very much. They can do that in their own bedroom or perhaps, they prefer that the bed is moved to a more common room, like a living room or den. In this way they can participate in the daily activities of the family. They may want to stay on the main floor for a while to avoid climbing any stairs. It may be helpful to have the bed near to a bathroom so the person does not have far to travel. Carpeted floors (not throw rugs) help make sure the person is less likely to slip and fall and also cuts down on noise. Being near a window and sunlight is very enjoyable for many people as well as being surrounded by favorite pictures, music and pets. The room should be comfortably warm or cool depending on the season, with good air ventilation (without causing drafts).

Some **furniture** that is helpful to have in arm's reach of a comfortable bed includes:

• A **small table** (the same height as the bed) for medication, snacks, radio, writing paper, etc. Even better is a table with a few drawers (like in a hospital) where a person can put some personal items like comb, brush, toothbrush, mirror, box of tissues, urinal or bedpan.

• A comfortable **armchair** nearby where they can sit, perhaps look out a window, watch television or read. The chair should be high enough so that it is easy to get in and out of.

- A sturdy **foot stool** to help the person get in and out of bed if the bed is too high.
- A small **bell, intercom or buzzer** to call for help.
- Something fresh to drink especially **water** and some favorite **snacks**.
- A **place to put** magazines, books, television converter, knitting or other leisure things.
- **Good lighting** for talking with people, reading, watching television.
- A sturdy **food tray** to help make eating more comfortable in bed.
- A **telephone**.

You may also need some special **equipment** to help you. Talk with your home care case manager to arrange for the things that you need to borrow, rent or buy. These may include:

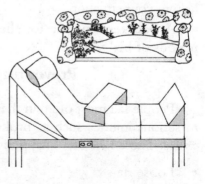

- An **adjustable bed** (similar to a hospital bed).
- A **bed table** high enough to fit over one's knees lying in bed.
- A **bed cradle** to protect a sensitive part of the body from the weight or movement of sheets and blankets.
- A **back rest** to help a person sit up in bed.
- **Sheepskin padding** or pillows, foam or sponge pads to help prevent bedsores.
- **Incontinence pads** for under the person in bed in case there is any urine or feces (stool) incontinence.

- A **footboard** made of strong cardboard, or hard pillow or something else quite creative to allow the person in bed to push against it so that they can keep their body position comfortable. Often people who are sitting up in bed end up sliding down the bed to uncomfortable positions.

**Adaptive devices** may be helpful such as:

- A **walker, wheelchair or canes** to help the person move about.
- A **commode** so the person does not have to use the bathroom.
- **Grab bars** along hallways when walking, on staircases, in bathrooms by the toilet and in the tub/shower, near the bed, etc.; wherever a person could use a bit of extra support with their balance and movement.
- There are many **simple aids** to help with lifting, reaching, and eating. Ask an occupational therapist for what might best help in your situation.
- A **backrest** specific for the person may help for long periods of bed rest.

## Preventing Falls

People fall most often in their own homes. This can lead to serious injuries such as broken hips in elders or broken wrists. These falls often happen because of:

- Loose rugs.
- Wet or slippery floors.
- Objects left on the floor (toys, magazines, paper).

Check with your physiotherapist or nurse about ways to make the home safe. If the person needs their home adapted for long-term care situations you might:

• Ask home care for side rails on the bed for someone who might fall out of bed.

• Install night lights so someone doesn't fall in the dark on the way to the bathroom or to get a snack from the kitchen.

• Install grab bars in the bathroom by the toilet, sink and in the bathtub/shower.

• Install handrails in hallways and staircases.

• Laying down non-slip mats in the bathroom, by the kitchen sink, in entranceways to the home where there is no carpet.

• Lower frequently used objects from upper shelves in kitchen, bathroom, bedroom and other common areas.

• Either get rid of throw rugs or secure them with tacks or two-sided tape.

• Make sure all electrical, telephone and other cords are under carpets or laid along the baseboards. If a cord must be in a pathway, secure it with wide tape.

• Put a slip-resistant floor finish on hardwood floors.

• Older people need better light to see so increase lighting in the home and have a flashlight by their bedside in case the power goes off.

• Make sure the layout of the furniture allows easy access to exits, hallways, telephones, etc. so a person does not need to move around too many objects in their daily movements.

# Basic Care

## The Mutual Gift of Caring

Caring for someone can be quite time consuming. Just reading the previous instructions may be enough to make you ask if you have what it takes to do this well. When I was caring for my parents, I was a recent university graduate in the fields of history and political science. I had no experience caring for anyone (including myself if the truth be told). Using some of these basic care skills that I learned from nurses, or through trial and error, I was amazed at how calming and enjoyable they were to use for my parents. These were intimate moments of real caring. Physical care of people we love is one of the greatest gifts we give to them and to ourselves. I would not have believed that if I had not experienced it. These are life-defining moments that make us better children, spouses, parents, friends and neighbors.

The people we care for may not remember what we said. They will remember how we make them feel and physical care is one of the most intimate forms of communication we ever experience.

In the days and weeks ahead you may be involved in a wide range of activities. You may be able to give another family member or friend some of the activities that you are less comfortable with while concentrating on your own strengths. However, you will likely have to do things you have never done before or do not feel comfortable doing at first. Give it a little time and you will be amazed at how quickly you learn.

# Preventing Further Illness

We were always told to wash our hands before meals for good reason. When caring for someone it is wise to wash your hands before touching them or their food in any way. This helps prevent infections from spreading from you to them and vice-versa. Wash with warm soapy water and dry thoroughly before and after physical contact. You may want to use a hand lotion to prevent dryness or chapping.

It may be wise to use disposable latex or vinyl gloves and a disposable apron if you are likely to touch blood or other body fluids. Dispose of the gloves, dirty dressings, apron, etc. in two plastic bags for extra safety to prevent the spread of infection or disease. Needles should not be thrown into the trash. Put them in a plastic or metal container (e.g. empty bleach bottle) and tape lid shut once the container is full to prevent needles from falling out accidentally. Check with your nurse about how best to dispose of the needle container.

It is likely in North America that someone will have a cold or flu in your home during the year. Use a mask to cover their mouths if they are coughing and wear one yourself if you need to near them. Children and pets also spread germs. Remind children about hand washing. Have pets checked by a veterinarian to make sure they are healthy with up-to-date shots. Be especially careful to wash your hands after cleaning up after your pet, cleaning out the litter box or bottom of the cage.

## Helping People Get Around

A good deal of your time may be spent helping the person get in or out of bed, walk around their home or helping them to the bathroom. You have seen relatively short nurses help people around the hospital so you know that you do not need to be very tall or physically strong. You do need to be smart about what you do so that you do not hurt yourself. Ask your home care coordinator/case manager to bring in an occupational therapist or physiotherapist for an in-house assessment. They are experts at helping you decide what assistive devices might be helpful and what types of support and care you can provide that would be most helpful to the person who needs it. Also ask your visiting home nurse for further tips.

**Note** The tips in this section apply best to people who are weak and need some extra support. They do not necessarily apply to people who have muscular or neurologic conditions or those who have had a stroke. Always check with a physiotherapist or occupational therapist or visiting home nurse before trying something new.

Here are some specific tips that might help as well:

• If movement causes extra pain, check with the physician or visiting home nurse about giving a pain relieving medication about 30 minutes before the movements happen (e.g., before daily baths, regular trips to the dining room).
• Keep your feet and toes pointed straight ahead with your weight evenly divided on both feet.
• You need to stand as straight as you can, keep your head up, shoulders down and knees slightly bent.
• When lifting someone, you should have your head, shoulders and hips form a straight line. You need to bend

your knees and keep your back as straight as possible when lifting. Have your feet about 30 cm (one foot) apart for the best stability.

• Learn a few stretching exercises for your legs, arms, back and stomach muscles and practice them before you do any lifting or assisting.

• The closer you are to the person or object you are lifting, the less strain on your muscles.

• Make sure the area you will be lifting or walking in does not have anything in the way (e.g., toys and throw rugs) and that it is not slippery.

• Wear comfortable, low heel shoes and loose fitting clothes.

• Use wheelchair breaks always to prevent people from losing their balance and falling.

• Remove the foot pedals on wheelchairs or move them to the side to give extra room.

## Moving Someone in Bed

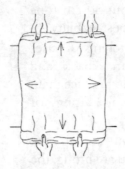

The greatest invention in the world (or so it seemed to me at the time I was taking care of my parents) is a draw sheet. This is just a regular sheet folded several times and placed sideways on the bed. The person lies on top with the sheet under their shoulders and hips. A person on either side of the bed grabs the sheet at the same time and together they lift the person up to move them closer to the head or the bottom of the bed. This is very helpful when someone is sitting up in bed and they keep sliding to the foot of the bed. If they cannot move themselves, the draw sheet is perfect to move them without a lot of pulling or pushing on their skin. You can also use the draw sheet to help turn someone onto their side by placing one end of the draw sheet over the person and pulling it towards you.

## Helping Turn Someone in Bed

Other than the draw sheet, you can also help a person turn in bed in the following way:

Have their far arm across their chest towards you.

Bend their far leg at the knee while their foot still rests on the mattress. Bring the bent leg towards you. As you do this, their far shoulder will naturally start to move towards you through the leverage of the leg. Reach over with your hand to guide their shoulder towards you comfortably and safely. This will put the person on their side with their bent knee giving extra security.

Place pillows to support their back and, if necessary, between their legs for added comfort. Adjust the head pillow as needed.

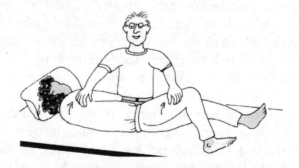

## Getting Someone Out of Bed and Into a Chair

Get a physiotherapist, occupational therapist or experienced nurse to show you the proper techniques for your specific situation. Also ask them about **transfer** and **walking belts** that can give you something to hold onto when helping the person move about. Remember, what you do for someone who is weak from surgery is not the same as what you might do for someone who has partial paralysis. The following are some general tips that can help you remember what you have been shown by a professional.

1. Put a safe and solid chair with arm rests next to the bed facing you. The chair should be high enough to make it easy for the person to get into it and out again.

2. Raise the head of the bed as high as it will go. Help move the person's legs over the side of the bed. If the bed is not adjustable, have them lay on their side, move their legs over the side of the bed and slip your closet hand under their neck and shoulder to support those parts as they lift up. Give them a moment to rest, as they may be a bit dizzy after lying down so long.

3. Help put the person's slippers or shoes on (or do it when they are still lying down if they cannot help).

4. If the bed is too high put a strong footrest by the bed to help the person step down comfortably.

5. Help the person slide forward to the edge of the bed so their feet are touching the floor or footstool.

6. Face the person with your foot that is nearest the chair one step behind the other. This will allow you to turn easily in the direction of the chair. Have the person put their hands on their knees to help them push up with their legs. Guide them with your hands around and under their buttocks and assist the person to stand on their own feet. If they need extra support, hold them under their

elbows as they hold your upper arms and lift together. If necessary, use two people to provide the support needed to lift the person and transfer them to a chair safely.

7.   Have the person brace themselves with their hands around your elbows while you hold them under their elbows for leverage.

8.   Help the person slide off the bed.

9.   Bend your knees and press your forward knee against the person's opposite knee. Let them catch their breath and balance themselves as they stand.

10.  Let the person shuffle backward towards the chair if they can and help them lower themselves. If they need help, pivot them using the pressure on their knee, and then lower them into the chair.

## From a Chair into Bed

Reverse the instructions from above making sure the person helps with as much of the moving as possible. As well, make sure the chair, footstool and bed won't move while you are helping the person.

## Walking

Help the person stand (as above) from their bed or a chair. You can offer extra support either by holding them under their arm or elbow or using a 'walking belt' or their own belt to grab onto for extra support.

When you walk together, have your closest arm around their waist and the other hand can hold their nearest elbow or hand for extra support. Stay close to the person so that your hip can give them extra stability.

**Note:** If the person can no longer stand and they begin to slowly slump onto the floor, bend your own knees and help them glide against your body and down your knee to the floor. They may have their legs in front of them and sitting down or their legs are under them and they are in a slumped kneeing position. After they

have rested, you can put a chair in front of them and help them kneel in front of it for support as you slowly bring them to a standing position. If their legs are out in front, help hem turn onto their knees. Let them rest their hands on the chair so they can push themselves up. (See below if they are too weak to push up on their own.) Help them put their strongest leg up with their foot flat on the floor and their knee bent. Use your arms under their armpits or using their belt to help while they use the chair to push themselves up. Bend at the knees and try to keep your back in good alignment (although this is difficult in this position). Lift up with your arm at the same time the person pushes up from the chair. Turn them slowly using their strong leg to pivot on. If they are using their right leg to pivot on, use your left hand to help them turn. Once in the chair, let them sit down for a more comfortable rest. If they cannot get up, wait for help to bring them back to bed or try to slide the chair to the bed. At all times, remember to safeguard your own back since you cannot be helpful if you injure yourself.

If the person is too weak to use both hands to push themselves up from the ground, have them use one hand on the chair and you use your strongest forearm under their remaining bent forearm. As they lift up from the ground using their bent pivot leg, you lift with your arm at the same time with your other arm 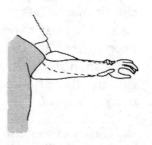 providing support at their belt or around their waist.

## Personal Care

### Using a Bedpan or Urinal

None of us enjoy having to use a bedpan or urinal. No matter how hard we try, it is an unnatural feeling and not all that comfortable. However, it is necessary sometimes. After you have helped the person with the equipment, give them some privacy and wait for them to call you for help again.

Leave a clean bedpan or urinal and toilet paper close to the bed so that people who are able can use it themselves and just call you when they are done.

## Specific Tips

Find out if they can use a commode beside the bed. A commode is a portable toilet that looks like a chair. It allows someone to go to the toilet without having to go to the bathroom. There are various types including ones on wheels and ones with removable armrests. Your visiting home nurse, home care case manager or family doctor can help you decide which is best.

**Note**: People who are receiving narcotic pain medication may have difficulty with bowel functions (e.g., with constipation). Talk to your family doctor or visiting home nurse right away to prevent the problem from getting worse. People need to continue using the right dose of pain medication so that they can remain relatively pain free and alert but they also need help controlling any side effects of that medication.

If they cannot use a commode, follow these tips:

1. Make sure you get the right kind of bedpan or urinal. There are different models for different purposes and you should get the kind that is most comfortable for your specific purpose. Plastic bedpans, vomit trays and the like are not as cold as metal ones.
2. Make sure the bedpan or urinal is clean, warm (you can rinse it with hot water), and dry.
3. Wash your hands thoroughly and dry them with a clean towel.
4. You may want to put some talcum powder on the top of the bedpan so it does not stick to a person's skin.

5. Once they are using the bedpan or urinal, you can raise the head of the bed to help them feel more comfortable. Make sure the foot of the bed is down so that urine will run into the urinal and not pour out by mistake.

6. Make sure the person is wiped clean and dry.

7. Cover the bedpan or urinal before removing it to prevent spilling. Empty in the toilet and clean. If you rinse with cold water and baking soda it helps keep the equipment odor free.

8. Wash your hands and help the person to wash theirs.

Urinating and having bowel movements in such a public way can be a major source of embarrassment and frustration for people. They should not have to wait to use the equipment or to have it taken away when they are done. Anything you can do to help people maintain their sense of control at this time will be an invaluable gift.

People do not have to have a bowel movement everyday to be healthy. It varies from person to person. They will know if the frequency of their bowel movements is normal or abnormal.

Menstruating women should have all the supplies and assistance they need. Again ask them what they need and what kind of help would be appreciated and who they prefer to help them.

## Helping Someone Onto a Bedpan

If they can help, have them lay on their back, bend their knees so their feet are flat on the mattress and ask them to lift their buttocks while you put the bedpan under them.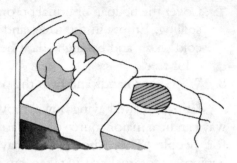

If they prefer, they can roll onto the bedpan. Have the person roll onto their side, place the bedpan against their buttocks and ask them to roll onto their back.

If they cannot lift themselves or roll onto a bedpan help them to roll onto their side. They will tell you how to help them. Place an incontinence pad on the mattress (if there is not one already), put the bedpan on the mattress in the correct spot (often a little dent in the mattress where the person was lying), and help them to roll onto the bedpan. You may need to adjust it a little for comfort.

## If Someone is Incontinent of Urine or Feces

Incontinence means that the person cannot control their bladder or bowel movements. Odor, infections or rashes may develop if the person does not regularly change and keep dry. Their skin care becomes especially important at this point to prevent painful bedsores and other uncomfortable skin conditions.

- Get specific advice from a dietician, visiting home nurse, home care case manager or your family doctor.
- Put a plastic sheet under the bottom sheet of the bed.

• Use incontinent pads or a clean towel under the person in bed. Change as needed. Reusable incontinence pads or towels should be placed in a sealable container until they are washed. Wash the container with a disinfectant and air out regularly to diminish odor. Sometimes having a vinegar and water solution in the container helps minimize odor as well. Non-reusable incontinence pads should be sealed into an airtight garbage bag and kept outdoors and away from the person's room. Oranges with cloves stuck in them, and left in the room, can also reduce odors. There are also commercial products to help with odor. Ask your visiting home nurse or home care case manager about suitable products for your situation.

• Make sure the person's skin remains clean and dry. Use soapy water and pat as needed. You may also want to use a water-resistant cream to protect the skin. Bedsores are extremely painful and dangerous. They are frequently the result of damp skin and poor blood circulation. Anything you do to keep the skin clean and dry helps a lot. You will also need to keep the bedclothes dry at all times.

• Pajama bottoms are not very practical. Long T-shirts, pajamas tops or oversized flannel shirts are quite comfortable. Socks may also help keep someone warm in cool temperatures.

• The person may want to use adult diapers to keep dry and comfortable and to allow them to get out of bed and walk around for exercise. Check to see if your local home care program covers these and other supplies.

## Helping with a Bath or Shower

When the person can go into the bath or shower you may find the following tips useful:

• Before the person goes into the bathroom, have all the things they will need ready. Run the bath and check the water for the person's preferred temperature. Have the soap, washcloth, shampoo and other items (razor blade, cream, etc.) nearby. Have the towels within easy reach. If possible, put the towels in the dryer for two minutes to warm them up so the person can feel warm when they dry themselves.

• Helping people to stand up or sit/lie down can be very difficult on your own body. It is important to remember all the rules of lifting and leaning over that you were taught in school. Remember to bend at the knees when you are picking up an object and keep your back as straight as possible. Remember as well, that the closer you are to the person or object you are lifting, the less strain you put on your lower back, arms and legs. Some regular squatting exercises will help strengthen your legs and lower back.

• If you get quite sore by helping someone get up or down, ask your family doctor, visiting home nurse, occupational therapist or chiropractor to give you clearer instructions of how to lift someone properly so that you do not continue to hurt yourself.

• Help the person into the bath or shower making sure you bend your knees slightly and keep your back as straight as you can. You may want to put a long towel under their arms to help lower them into the bath.

- If the person is able to help themselves more, you can help them sit on the side of the tub (on a warm, non-slip towel or mat), swing their legs over and help them to ease into the tub. Reverse the procedure when they want to get out.

- Make sure the bath or shower has a non-slip bath mat.

- If the person needs help for weeks or months, it may be wise to adapt your bath or shower with handles and other safety aids. Check with an occupational therapist or physiotherapist through your home care program.

- If the person prefers a shower, rent or borrow a bath chair or use a water-resistant chair so they can sit down comfortably. Your home care program may be able to arrange this.

- The person may feel more comfortable if their genital area is covered. You can use a short apron or modified towel with Velcro tabs so the person has the privacy they want.

### Giving a Bed Bath

Bed baths may be a little (or a lot) embarrassing for someone. However, they are necessary for people who cannot take a bath or shower. The person must stay clean and dry throughout the day and night. Bed baths can be quite comforting because they allow a little exercise, improve blood circulation and also provide an opportunity for gentle massage and a chat if the person enjoys that. They also give you a chance to check for bedsores, bruises, rashes and other skin conditions. Bed baths are an intimate experience and must be done with respect and compassion. They should not be rushed. You may even want some music playing in the background for mutual enjoyment.

My father and I were very shy the first time we helped wash my mother in bed. We didn't know what we were doing so my father and I washed her from top to bottom, all at once. Then we dried her from top to bottom, all at once. She froze. We learned to **wash and dry one part at a time and keep the rest covered for warmth.** She was so patient with us.

## *What You Need*

- ❑   A large bowl or basin filled with hot water (hot enough to be warming).
- ❑   Mild soap.
- ❑   Skin lotion, cream and/or powder.
- ❑   Washcloths (for washing and rinsing) and towels.
- ❑   Personal toiletries: comb, brush, tooth brush and paste, nail file and clippers, make-up, deodorant, shaving items, perfume/cologne (whatever the person needs).
- ❑   A suitable change of clothing.

## *What You Do*

•   Wash your hands thoroughly and try to make the room temperature comfortably warm or cool depending on the season.

•   Let the person do as much as possible for themselves. If they cannot do much themselves:

•   Wash one body part at a time starting at the face and working down or in the reverse direction; whichever the person prefers. The rest of the body should be covered with the top bed sheet or a large warm towel.

•   During a bed bath, you may also put a basin of water on a towel at the foot of the bed so the person can soak one foot at a time in the basin. It is very comforting. Dry the feet when they are finished.

•   Wash carefully under the skin folds since these are the most likely spots for rashes or other skin problems. This is especially true under the arm, in the groin area, buttocks, stomach skin folds, and under a woman's breasts. In sensitive areas, the person may be able to help with the washing more than in other areas.

- Cleaning the back is the perfect opportunity to give someone a back rub whether they are on their stomach or on their side. Once you have cleaned them you can use skin lotion to evenly massage the upper and lower back and buttocks. Ask the person how they like their backs rubbed best and follow their lead. Use soft pressure and move your hands in circular motions. Do it 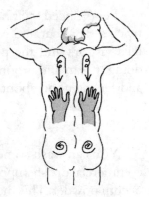 several times, always keeping your hands on the person's skin and using enough lotion so that your hands move smoothly. You can also do this while a person is sitting at a table leaning over and resting their head on a pillow. This may be very helpful for people who cannot lay on their stomach or sides for very long e.g., elders or people who have had recent surgery or have breathing problems.

- People often enjoy having their face, temples, neck, hands, elbows, feet and heels massaged as well. Again follow their wishes.

- Once you have completely washed and dried the person, help them with their personal hygiene. For example, they may want to use deodorant, put on some makeup, have their hair combed, etc.

- Help them put on their clothes in whatever way they ask.

## General Care of Hair

People need their hair cleaned, combed/brushed (at least twice a day), cut and set. The condition of one's hair often tells visitors and the person themselves how well they are doing. Clean and groomed hair is important for good health and feeling good about yourself.

### Dry Shampoo

You can wash someone's hair using 'dry' shampoo like a commercial dry shampoo, cornstarch or natural (unperfumed) talcum powder. This method was all the rage in the late 1960s and early 1970s for teenagers -- I remember it well!

For someone who needs their hair washed in bed, dry shampoo can sometimes be a quick alternative to a normal wash. Do the following:

- Place a towel under the person's head.
- Sprinkle powder on the scalp and massage the hair and scalp gently.
- Brush the powder out of the hair with slow, even strokes. If hair is tangled, hold the hair near the scalp before brushing through to the end.
- Wash the hairbrush after each dry shampooing.

### Wet Shampoo

If the person needs a normal hair wash but cannot use the bath or shower you can wash their hair in bed. You will need:

❑   A plastic sheet to protect the bed.
❑   A waterproof cape (like in a hair salon) or a plastic garbage bag with a hole for the head and cut along the sides to make a cape.

❑   A jug or pitcher of warm-to-hot water (several if the
    person has long hair).
❑   A bucket or large basin to collect water, (there are also
    special shampoo trays available through some drug
    stores).
❑   A washcloth or small towel, plus two larger towels for
    drying.
❑   Pillow(s).
❑   Shampoo.
❑   Comb or brush.
❑   A hair dryer (if needed).

### To Help The Person Wash Their Hair If They Cannot Do It Themselves

1.   You may want to put a towel or plastic sheet on the
     floor under the bucket to catch any spilled water.
2.   Have the person lie on their back with their head over
     the side of the bed (adjust pillows, covers, etc. so they
     are comfortable).
     Put the bucket or
     basin on a small
     table under the
     person's hair.
3.   Cover the area with
     the plastic sheet and
     have the person wear their cape with the back side
     covering their pillow rather than tucked under them.
4.   Pour warm water from the jug over their hair so that the
     water falls in the bucket or basin below.
5.   Put the shampoo into the hair and gently massage it in to
     lather the hair and scalp.
6.   Rinse the hair with the remaining water.
7.   Dry the hair with a towel and then with the dryer if
     necessary.

8. Empty the bucket and tidy up the bed. Remove the cape and plastic sheet. Place the other dry towel on the pillow to soak up any moisture still in the hair.

9. Other tasks like setting or coloring the hair can be done in bed using the same common sense approach to comfort and cleaning as described here.

## Taking Care of Someone's Back

Many people like a back rub whether they get a bed bath or not. If the person agrees, you can give them a back rub while they lie on their stomach or on their side just as in the diagram earlier. Use a good skin lotion or experiment with natural oils such as rose or almond oil. Check with the visiting home nurse or family doctor for suggestions.

If the person cannot turn in bed themselves, they need to be turned every two hours or so. Otherwise there is too much pressure on just one part of their skin and they may get painful bedsores. Use pillows to provide the back support they need when they are on their side. Earlier in the book there are illustrations that show proper back support in different lying positions.

## Other Areas Needing Care

Most people can brush their own teeth (or soak them), clean their mouths, ears and nose. Some people may need a little bit of help; let them tell you how you can best help. They may need extra help especially with their fingernails. For example, you might brighten up a woman's day by helping them use their favorite nail polish.

Feet and toenails may require a good footbath (with the person sitting in a chair or lying in bed with the basin on the mattress). It is important to clean and dry between the toes as well as the rest of the foot. They may need a cream to help prevent skin dryness. This is a good time to check their toenails. They should be trimmed in the same shape as their toes without sharp edges to prevent damage to other toes and ingrown nails.

## Adaptive Clothing

If someone must stay in bed for a long time or if they must stay around the home for long periods they may wish to adapt some of their clothes to make care easier on themselves and for others.

For example, rather than long pants or pajamas bottoms, they may wear oversized shirts or pajamas tops that are buttoned in front to keep their upper and lower body warm while also making it easier to get dressed and undressed. Sometimes, the back part of a shirt or pajamas top can get wrinkled and be quite uncomfortable for someone in bed for a long time. It may be worth taking some older shirts/pajamas tops and cutting up the back and sewing a seam on each side (much like those wonderful hospital gowns everyone loves to wear). Use a strip of extra cloth to make a tie at the top and middle if you like. You can also use oversized shirts/ pajamas tops and put them on backwards for a similar effect although it may not fit as nicely and may need a little cutting and sewing to fit better around the neck.

Scarves (light or heavy) may be very useful to make sure that someone remains warm if there is a draft. Also scarves can be used to keep one's head warm if the person has lost their hair during treatments. The book *Changes, Choices and Challenges* (in the reference section) gives examples of the creative uses of scarves. Socks or good slippers will also help keep feet warm.

# Bed Care

## Supported Lying Positions

People need to rest in different lying positions so that they do not put too much pressure on any single body part or skin area. People can sit up, lay down or lay on their sides as they normally do for sleeping.

### Sitting Up

The head should be raised about 45 to 60° with small pillows under their head, lower back and under their knees (or raise the foot portion of the bed). This position is helpful for eating, using a bedpan or urinal and helps improve how the person's heart and lungs work. If the person likes a large pillow, place it lengthwise to support their  upper back, shoulders and head. It may help to have a footboard at the bottom of their feet to allow them to push up a little as they will naturally slide down in bed over time.

### Lying Down

With the person in the center of the bed, put a pillow under their shoulders, neck and head. Another pillow can go under their lower back for extra support and a rolled up towel or smaller pillow under their ankles and knees. The person may also enjoy pillows under the upper arms and hands. Follow the person's wishes and change pillow positions as requested.

## Lying on the Side

When you look at a person lying on their side you should see the same body position as if they were standing with one leg bent up. The back is in line with the straight leg with pillows under the head, top arm and bent leg. Pillows can also be rolled along the person's back for extra support to prevent them from rolling onto their back when they are sleeping.

## Making a Bed

People may spend a lot of time in bed. It is important that the bed stay clean, dry and comfortable.

### Making an Unoccupied Bed

It seems silly to have a section on making a bed. Add to that that my mother would be amazed that I am offering advise on this subject at all and you get the idea that you should accept or reject any of the following advice based on your own expertise. However, many of us have never had to make a bed for someone who will spend days there. How you make the bed will decide how comfortable the person may be.

Try to use fitted bottom sheets so that the sheet has few wrinkles in it. Wrinkles add extra pressure to the person's skin and may cause bedsores. If you can, try to make the bed when the person is normally out of bed (e.g., taking a bath, sitting in a chair). Try to avoid extra efforts to get the person out of bed so that you can change it. The more natural the effort, the less trouble for everyone.

## Making an Occupied Bed

Sometimes the person cannot get out of bed while you change the sheets. This takes a little more planning but is quite simple after a few tries. The idea is to make one side of the bed at a time. It is harder to explain what you need to do than to actually do it. After you have done this once or twice you will master the steps and fill in the little details that are most important to you and your loved ones.

1. Make sure you have all the clean sheets, pillowcases, etc. that you need on a chair beside the bed.
2. If possible, have the bed lying flat (if it is adjustable) and the person using only one pillow.
3. Place another chair on the opposite side of the bed you are working on. If you are using a hospital bed, you can raise the side rail on the far side. Either way will allow the person in bed to hold onto something as they roll onto their side closest to the chair. Their back should face you and they should be covered with a top sheet, blanket or cover so they can stay warm.
4. Loosen the bottom sheet at the head and foot end of the bed, as well as any top sheets and blankets. Roll the bottom sheet as close to the person's back as possible. They will have to roll over this old sheet and the new one when you are ready.
5. Smooth out the mattress cover.
6. Lay down the clean fitted bottom sheet, folded lengthwise, from head to foot ends of the bed. Tuck in the head and foot ends and smooth out the sheet as much as possible.

7. Roll the remaining bottom sheet, lengthwise, as close to the person's back as possible. It will be right beside the old bottom sheet.

8. Ask (or help) the person roll toward you, over the sheets. If they need extra support, have them roll onto their back  first, lift their far leg towards you gently, and help them roll onto their side facing you. Bring the chair from the other side to put where you were standing or lift the hospital bed's side rail so that the person has something to hold onto and help them from falling out of bed.

9. Move to the other side of the bed. Loosen the old bottom sheet and pull it completely off the bed as well as pulling the new sheet from under the person. Some of the sheets might get caught under the body weight of the person in bed but just pull gently until they are loose. If necessary, gently push the bottom part of the person's back to release some of the body weight on the sheets. Smooth the mattress cover.

10. Tuck in the new bottom sheet at the head and foot of the bed and make sure there are few, if any, wrinkles.

11. Have the person lie on their back and position the bed comfortably for them. Replace old pillowcases.

12. If the person uses a duvet, replace the outside cover as needed.

13. If the person uses sheets and blankets they will already be untucked from replacing the bottom sheets. Place a clean sheet on top of the blanket. Have the person hold onto the blanket and clean sheet as you pull out the old top sheet from the foot of the bed. If they cannot help you,

you will have to do this yourself and take a little more time.

14. Turn the sheet and blanket around so that the blanket is on top, tuck in the top sheet, blankets, and bed spread (if they like).

**Extra Tips:** Sometimes there may be other things on the bottom sheet that will need to be changed or at least kept there. For example, draw sheets, sheepskin pads and incontinence pads are often used for someone who is in bed. The same principles apply as in the instructions above. You do one side of the bed at a time and the person rolls over the old and new items you are changing. The more things there are, the higher the 'bump' the person has to roll over.

# Pain and Symptom Control

## Describing Pain and Symptoms

Pain is a very subjective sensation. One person's headache may force him to bed while another person's headache may allow her to continue to work. The following checklist will allow you to describe your pain and other symptoms as clearly as possible. If you or a family member/friend can, write down the answers for your doctor.

Where in the body did the pain/symptom begin?
When did it start (date and time)?
On a scale of 1-10, with 10 equaling the worst pain you have ever had (e.g., broken arm, back pain, severe toothache), how do you rate your pain?
Describe any other symptoms you have had.
What were you doing at the time of the pain/symptom?
To what degree does your pain/symptom limit your normal activities?
How long does the pain/symptom last (an hour, all day)?

Is the pain/symptom constant or does it change?
Does the pain/symptom stay in one place or spread out to other parts of your body?
What makes the pain/symptom worse?
What makes the pain/symptom better?
Other information.

## Pain Control Medication

Pain has different degrees of intensity. Pain control experts divide pain into: mild, moderate, severe, very severe and overwhelming. At present, experts recommend the following types of medication for each level of pain:

Mild: A non-narcotic e.g., aspirin (ASA).
Moderate: A weak narcotic e.g., codeine.
Severe: An intermediate-strength narcotic e.g., increased dose of codeine.
Very severe: A potent narcotic e.g., morphine.
Overwhelming: A potent narcotic and sedative e.g., diazepam.

It takes time and experimentation to arrive at the exact combination of medications that will keep a patient pain-free and alert. Patients and families can shorten this process by recording any positive or negative results of new medications and talking to their doctor about these results.

## Other Pain Control Techniques

There are other treatments for pain control. A few of these techniques use medications in a different way or use other forms of therapy such as:

***Radiotherapy*** Radiation is used to shrink tumors to reduce a patient's symptoms.

***Nerve blocks*** For localized acute cancer pains, a local anesthetic or neurolytic injection is given to block nerves from sending pain messages to the brain. Results may be temporary or long-lasting.

*Hypnosis*  A hypnotist can use oral suggestion to sometimes increase a person's pain threshold.

*Acupuncture*  This ancient Chinese art uses sterile needles in very specific spots to neutralize pain messages going to the brain.

*Neurosurgery*  With the proper use of medication and other techniques, the need for neurosurgery should be uncommon. If other measures do not work, neurosurgery should not be delayed.

## Symptom Control Techniques

Total pain is not only the sensation or feeling of pain. Total pain is a combination of physical and psychological feelings. The primary psychological component of total pain is fear. Fear can aggravate a patient's physical pain, so fear, anxiety and other negative emotions must also be treated. Add to this list diarrhea, constipation, lack of hunger and energy, bedsores, lack of mobility and other symptoms and you will understand the need for symptom control and relief.

Some of the symptom control and stress management techniques that home care personnel use, other than medications, include:

*Diet*  Some foods cause constipation while others cause loose stool. Knowing which foods cause what reaction can help caregivers to alleviate a specific symptom.

*Exercise*  Extended bed rest can lead to bed sores, constipation, back aches, general immobility and loss of muscle strength because of the decreased use of muscles. Exercises, active or passive, can be done by the patient or with someone's help in bed or they can be done when the patient is out of bed. Walking, stretching and breathing are excellent forms of exercise.

**Skin care** Nurses that visit patients at home will often tell you that bedsores are one of their greatest concerns. Bedsores are very painful and almost always avoidable. They occur most often when elbows, ankles, shoulders, hips, buttocks, heels and the back are in constant contact with a surface. Paralyzed or unconscious patients are most likely to get bedsores. Proper skin care includes daily washing, skin cream treatments and the use of a lamb or sheep's skin mattress covering or water-circulating mattress pad. For people unable to move themselves in bed it is important to change their body position at least every two hours to avoid bedsores.

**Massage** Gets the blood circulating, invigorates the skin and can be very soothing and or exhilarating depending on the type of massage. Everyone enjoys a massage so it is not a surprise that they are excellent for the physical and emotional well being of a patient as well.

**Recreational therapy** Physical activity like a walk in the garden or a card game with friends encourages people to make decisions and participate in things that they have always enjoyed.

**Art therapy** People can express feelings by doing creative work. Whatever the person decides to may end up as a gift to a grandchild or a cherished memento for a family member or caregiver.

**Music therapy** People can relax and be comforted by playing, listening, interpreting, and talking about music. Personal preferences are important to the success of music therapy -- just playing favorite music can be therapeutic.

**Laughter** Technically it increases the production of endorphins (natural chemical pain killers in our bodies), reduces tension, distracts attention, changes expectations, and is an internal jog of organs for exercise. In another sense, laughter is contagious and lets people express their feelings in a less threatening way. It can change the mood of a place faster than any other emotion. Find a few good records or videos of comedians like Bill Cosby and sit back and enjoy yourself.

***Relaxation exercises***   Deep breathing, visualization, hypnosis, meditation and prayer are all ways to relax. They help to relax the body physically and mentally.

***Listening***   Perhaps no method of symptom control has a greater impact on a patient's fear, anxiety, loneliness and depression than someone who listens unconditionally and answers questions in an honest way.

The purpose of all of these techniques is to give people a sense of control over their lives. Even if they are bedridden, decisions have to be made about exercises, diets and other daily living tasks. Making decisions about their care helps to give patients a sense of control. Independence is very important to people and symptom control helps them to be as independent for as long as possible.

# What Prevents Adequate Pain and Symptom Control?

## Errors by the Person Receiving Care

- Believing the pain and symptoms are untreatable.
- Not contacting the doctor for help.
- Telling the doctor and family that the pain isn't strong or the symptoms aren't bad.
- Failing to take medication.
- Taking the medication at the wrong times or not consistently.
- Fearing drug addiction or drug tolerance.

- Believing pain killers are only for extreme pain.
- Discontinuing medication because of severe side effects and not telling the doctor.

### Doctors or Nurses' Errors

- Ignoring a patient's description of pain and symptoms because it sounds extreme.
- Not seeing through the patient's brave face.
- Prescribing medications that are too weak.
- Giving medication only when the person says her pain has returned (effective pain control prevents the return of pain).
- Believing post-surgery pain killers are suitable for cancer pain (generally, surgical pain is acute but short-lasting while cancer pain is chronic and can increase over time).
- Not giving enough information about the medication, its use and when it must be taken.
- Not knowing enough about different types of medication and how to move from one to another as the pain increases.

To deal with pain and symptoms, we must recognize that pain and symptoms are always real and unique for each person. Proper pain control requires the right drug or treatment, in the right way, and at the right time. Proper pain control includes some experimentation to discover the right combination of medication and treatments, requiring the complete co-operation of the patient, the family and the caregivers. When the pain is under control, other symptoms can be addressed, so that the patient's suffering is reduced and he can remain alert and active for as long as possible.

## Helping with Medication

The three biggest problems with taking medication (drugs) are: (1) that some people take far too many different ones without knowing how they react with each other, (2) they take the wrong kind of drugs or (3) they take too little of a drug for it to be helpful. For drugs to work best, people must:

- Use the right drug.
- In the right amount.
- At the right time.
- Buy the right method: liquid, tablets, drops (for ears, eyes and nose), ointment, sprays, suppositories, injections.
- Make sure they work well with any other drugs they are taking.

Whenever you see your doctor, go to a clinic or to an emergency department, make sure to have a current list of all your medications, how often you take them and what dose you take. This helps to spot any oversights in the amount and kind of medication you are taking. If you do not have a list, bring all your medications with you in the containers you got from the pharmacist.

Pharmacists are very knowledgeable about drugs and how they react with other medications. When you get a prescription filled, ask the pharmacist about side effects, mixing with other drugs (have a list of your drugs with you) and any tips on how you can help the person take their drugs in the right way. Also ask if there are any foods, drinks or personal habits that might affect the usefulness of the medication. For example, ask if one should not have alcohol with this medication or should not drive after taking it. Medications do affect people mentally and physically. People may have behavior changes, hallucinations or other mild to severe reactions. You have to be very careful to make sure the medications are more helpful than harmful.

If you forget to give a drug at the right time, check with your doctor or pharmacist about what to do. Do not double the dose at the next scheduled time without their permission, as this might be dangerous.

**Note**: If you are taking complementary therapies like vitamins, herbs, or are on a special diet, tell your doctor or pharmacist. For example, some Chinese herbs may be harmful when combined with certain medications.

## Medication Records

You may be taking several drugs and your prescriptions may change from time to time. The following record allows you to keep track of your drugs, what dose should be taken, at what time, with what conditions (e.g., take one hour before a meal, only with milk), and how well the drugs are working. The prescription date and the doctor's name are useful in emergency situations when your regular doctor may not be available to help you.

Make up your own chart on some separate pages. The following is a sample of how it might look. Change it to meet your own needs.

| Date | Drug | Dose | Taken | Doctor | Results/Side Effects |
|------|------|------|-------|--------|----------------------|
| Aug 1 | Tylenol 3 | 10 mg | 4 times a day | Kildair | Pain relieved after 5 hours but returned three weeks later. |
| Aug 23 | Tylenol 3 | 20 mg | 4 times a day | Kildair | Pain relieved after 6 hours. |

If you are taking various drugs, a **_Medication Table_** is useful to help you remember what to take, when and with what special instructions (e.g., with milk, during a meal). Use a pencil to fill in the drugs since they may change over time and you do not want to rewrite a whole list each time.

| Time | Drug(s) | Special Instructions |
|------|---------|----------------------|
| 8:00 a.m. | Give drug names, dose and color (e.g., yellow pills). | Take yellow pills with milk |
| 4:00 p.m. | Give drug names, dose and color (e.g., yellow pills). | Do not drive after taking pink liquid |
| 10:00 p.m. | Give drug names, dose and color (e.g., yellow pills). | Take drugs before bedtime. |

Make up your own schedule. Under the time column, list all the different times of the day that you need to take drugs. Some drugs you will only need to take once a day while another one might be every 4, 8 or 12 hours.

Local pharmacists often sell 'Dosettes'. These boxes have many small compartments and they can be used to prepare medication for a day or a few days at a time. They are very helpful in reminding people what to take at what time of day.

# Home Care Suggestions

There are many books listed in the reference section on the subject of home care and what family members can do and learn to make the situation more comfortable for everyone involved. The following are a few suggestions:

• Remember that people do not change much in character because of their illness. If they were easy going, caring and enjoyed a good joke before their illness they will probably be the same now. If they were unsatisfied with their lives, not easy to please and uncommunicative, they will probably not change a great deal because they are dying. Therefore treat them respectfully and give them the opportunity to direct your involvement in their care.

• Do not try to force someone to eat. People need control over their lives and should be encouraged to make their own decisions. Patients know that food is important to living. Their diet may be prescribed but a hot plate, small cooler or refrigerator by the bed allows them to eat many small meals when they are hungry. Also have lots of liquids available. If the person needs some help with eating, remember to keep common courtesies as part of the help. Do not make them go too fast or too slow. Give them a proper napkin and place setting, if possible. Remember that older people's tongues change shape and they must be fed differently than young children or adults.

• If conditions permit, encourage patients to decide if they wish to smoke, drink, walk around and have visitors. Even if these activities are tiring or unhealthy, the decision must rest with the person who is dying unless it harms someone else.

• Although family members often want to do what is best for their loved one, they must not forget about themselves. If you feel like you are being used, say so. If you are uncomfortable with decisions that the ill person has made, be honest about your feelings and arrange for someone else to help.

• Have a bell or other device available so that people in bed feel they have direct access to you. An ability to make contact, at their discretion, is crucial for the emotional support of people who are ill.

• Have music and television available. People who are great sports fans, for example, may benefit from a channel that has sports most of the day. This may be a great distraction from what is happening to them physically.

• Perhaps you can move the bed to the living room, den or other area where the person who is ill feels more a part of the family and every day living situations. If you live in a multi-level home you might move the patient to a ground floor room. If the bed is near a window the person can see what is going on outside;

• If the person needs to stay in bed for a long time, get a hospital-style bed or raise the one you have so that the people helping do not hurt their backs.

• For the caregivers at home, get all the help you need from your family, friends and professionals. Most people do not know what to do under these circumstances so they need to know how they can be helpful at this important time. Ask for specific help with chores, errands or providing care to your loved one.

- If the person is chronically or terminally ill, you may want to buy or borrow a home care book specifically for your situation. See the references listed at the back of this book for suggestions. Visit our Web site for free information at www.legacies.ca

Helping a loved one at home sometimes requires you to act as their spokesperson or advocate. When you work with the health care providers (e.g., doctors, nurses or pharmacists) make sure that:

- The person is properly fed the prescribed food on time.
- The person's medication and treatment is accurate and given at the proper times.
- Any tests or examinations have been approved.
- The doctor and other caregivers communicate with your loved ones and you about all matters.
- The person is given a sense of control and respect.

# Family and Friends: Visiting Someone Who Is Ill Or Recovering

Many family members and friends find it difficult to visit someone who is very ill. If the person is at home, it may be more difficult for some family members and friends overcome their fear of illness to visit because they assume that home visiting is less important than hospital visiting.

It is natural to hesitate to see someone you love who is recovering from an illness or who is seriously ill. Here are some suggestions that may help visitors:

• If you care about the person then go and visit, even if you are not great friends (e.g., a colleague from work).

• Check with the person or family to see when the best time is to visit. You don't want 20 people coming one day and no one coming the next.

• Remember that the people you love have not changed. They may be your parent, your child or a dear friend. Their personality, the qualities you admire and love, have not changed because they are ill or tired. Respect them rather than baby them. Include them in decisions. Ask their advice.

• There is nothing as comforting as a touch for many people. If the person will allow you and if you feel comfortable yourself, sit close to the person, hold their hand and give them a hug. Your touch and the caring in your eyes express more than words ever can.

• Use open-ended questions to permit people to decide what they want to talk about (if they want to talk at all). Questions like: "How are you feeling today?" "Are you comfortable?" "I love you so much. Is there anything I can do or say that will help?"

- Perhaps you can show or give this book to a family member or a friend to help them understand better what is happening to them and to the people around them. A small section of the book may open up the discussion in a non-threatening way. A book like this left with a person may or may not be read but it provides information to people who are naturally curious.

- Don't prepare a speech. Admit your fear of illness or sick people. The person needs to feel useful and if you are honest, they may help you overcome some of your fear so that you can have a really good visit.

- Be yourself. Act as you always do with the person. If you are naturally quiet then avoid telling all the latest jokes from work. If you normally gossip about old friends then continue to do so. If you are naturally outgoing don't become somber and serious. People need stability in their lives and family and friends can offer the greatest emotional stability.

- Let the patients vent their anger, frustration and despair. Their feelings are real and they need to get them out. It may have nothing to do with their illness but could be their treatment, their employer's attitude, old friends who no longer visit, or an acquaintance who owes them money but is nowhere to be seen. Offer to help if you can help improve the situation.

- It is often not helpful to compare the person with other people who have gone through similar things. It minimizes their unique experience and feelings.

- It is all right to cry and show your own feelings. You don't have to be strong all the time, for that makes the person dependent on your strength. If you cry and allow the person to be strong it is a normal relationship and one that benefits both of you.

- Don't hide behind a gift or card. It is your presence that is the gift. You can send a card or gift if you cannot visit, or between visits, to let the person know you are thinking of her.

- Try not to stay too long. Two short visits are better than one long one. This is especially true if the person tires easily.

- Remember the other family members. They need your emotional support, too, and practical things like transportation, food, baby-sitting and running errands can reduce their stress and provide them with the precious gift of time.

# Good Nutrition

It makes sense that what goes into the body affects how well a body heals itself or comforts itself. Good eating habits and good nutrition can make a world of difference to how one feels and heals. The book, *What to Eat When You Don't Feel Like Eating*, is an excellent, short cookbook of healing recipes for all people, but especially those who are sick. You must also remember how important it is to keep drinking during the day so that you do not become dehydrated during an illness. Some things to keep in mind about healthier and more enjoyable eating:

• We all have different nutritional needs, tastes and appetites. When anyone is ill, the needs may have to be adapted to what the person can tolerate or even enjoy. Some children may not be able to eat very much but might have something from their favorite fast food restaurant. It may not be perfect but it is a beginning.

• Someone's appetite depends on their physical condition, level of exercise and other distractions. Someone with little to do but watch television may begin to eat larger amounts of unhealthy food that they normally would not eat. Provide delicious alternatives.

• Medication, poor teeth, chronic fatigue and one's overall condition may affect the appetite and taste buds. Simple oral hygiene can improve one's joy of food. Encouraging regular brushing is still important when someone is ill or recovering from a condition.

• A well-balanced diet includes food from different food groups--**proteins** from fish, poultry, meat, and eggs; **milk and milk products; fruits and vegetables;** and **whole grain breads and cereals**. From a good combination of these groups, one gets the nutrition, vitamins and minerals necessary for healthier living.

• People need different amounts of food. They may need more from one food group depending on their condition. Some people need to eat healthier to regain strength. Athletes require more bulk from whole grain breads, pasta and cereals. People weakened from too little food over a long period of recovery need to eat higher calorie meals. *During or after a prolonged illness or recovery, it is necessary to speak with a dietician or other knowledgeable person about what foods, and in what quantities, the person should eat.* People should be able to eat what they enjoy as well as what is 'good for them.' A balanced diet allows for sweets, snacks and desserts in moderation. People may also enjoy something completely new since they will have no memory of this food affecting them badly like their more familiar foods.

• Serving meals should, when possible, include meals that are not all the same color (e.g., all yellow vegetables, white potatoes, applesauce and pale meat). Making the meal visually pleasing may encourage a healthier appetite. Dishes, the food tray and napkins should be clean. The food tray should rest comfortably on the person's lap or on a small bed tray.

• Some people prefer, or need, smaller meals offered more often than the standard three meals a day. For example, someone might benefit from smaller portions of food every 2-3 hours with snacks by the bedside during the night. It is better to offer less, than too much. Too large a portion can be overwhelming, and literally, nauseating.

• Any little thing you can do to add to the joy of a meal is a gift. For example, bringing the morning paper with breakfast, having a flower on the tray with lunch or giving a puzzle for a child to play with after dinner.

• Eating is often a social gathering. The person who is in bed may enjoy the company of others with them rather than eating alone. For example, for people who have difficulty eating enough calories each day, conversation, review of everyone's day and general social activity may encourage them to eat more than they had originally thought they could.

• People often have very particular habits around their meals. These should be followed as much as possible. For example, assist someone who likes to 'dress for dinner' with grooming. If they enjoy some background music, try to make this available in their room.

• Help people wash their hands before and after a meal. Wash your own hands as well before and after handling any food to help prevent the spread of germs. Be especially careful to cook meats and eggs thoroughly; wash raw vegetables and fruits; use hot water and soap to clean dishes, glasses, cooking utensils and your cutting board.

• If the person can come to the dining table, encourage them to do so. If they need to stay in their room, you might set up a card table or other temporary table there. If the person needs to remain in bed, make sure their back is well supported with pillows while they are in the sitting position.

• If the person needs help with cutting their meal and/or with feeding, remember they are not a baby and, therefore, should be helped in the most respectful and relaxed way possible. The person should continue to feel as a valued member of the family rather than a patient that needs help to eat. Follow the person's lead so you are helping them in ways that are supportive and comfortable.

• When helping someone to eat, the food should be bite size. Spoons should only be two-thirds full. *Older people's tongues* are shaped differently and, therefore, should not be spoon fed in the same way as younger people. Put smaller amounts in the side of their mouth and ensure the person swallows twice before giving more food to avoid the person choking on their food. Straws that bend near the top can be very helpful to minimize spills. The pace should be leisurely. Clear the tray away as soon as the meal is finished.

- Sitting up as straight as possible at the table or in bed with the head leaning forward is very helpful in preventing choking. The airway is more relaxed and open in this position. If possible, have the person sit up for about 30 minutes after the meal to encourage good digestion and minimize food coming back up.

- If the person is having trouble swallowing liquids or food, speak with a professional. They may recommend that you thicken liquids to trigger the "swallowing reflex" and to put food in a blender to make it easier to swallow. Ensure the person swallows twice to get any food that may be caught at the back of the palate or throat.

- The room where the person is eating should be at a comfortable temperature.

- The food and drink should be the right temperature for the person. Warn the person if any food or drink is very hot. Check to see if it is possible for the person to have their usual wine, coffee or other drinks with their meals.

# Talking With Your Doctor And Other Caregivers

## Understanding the Doctor and Other Professional Caregivers

There is a natural apprehension by many toward anything medical. In the past few years, however, there has been a heightened awareness that everyone benefits when the person and family work together with their professional caregivers. Open and honest communication relieves the person and family's anxiety, while the doctors and caregivers feel more job satisfaction and less personal stress.

Caregivers have stresses that everyone can help diminish by working together. For example, the stresses of many professional caregivers include:

- Heavy workload (it isn't enough to be a health care provider these days; you must also be a business person, a politician and a bureaucrat).
- Deciding how much patients should know about their illness (although most people prefer to know the truth about their illness, there are those who prefer that the doctor not tell them the complete truth).
- The increasing administrative requirements of governments and insurance companies.
- Little time to learn new treatments and methods even though some professionals (e.g., doctors) must study a certain number of hours per year to keep their license.
- Little time for personal stress reduction.
- Increasing numbers of lawsuits.
- A decreased public respect for medical professionals in general.

Some eminent doctors have written about doctor-patient relationships. Sir William Osler, 19th-century Canadian doctor, diagnostician and scholar believed that it is more important to know what type of patient has a disease rather than what type of disease a patient has. He gave his patients little medication but lots of optimism.

Norman Cousins in his book, *The Anatomy of an Illness,* describes a visit he had with Dr. Albert Schweitzer in Africa. Schweitzer explained his philosophy of medical practice. He believed that people carry their own doctor inside of them. They go to a doctor because they do not recognize their own strength. A doctor's greatest asset is their ability to bring out the doctor within each patient. By helping patients gain a sense of personal control over their lives, doctors can also have a professional satisfaction that they are making a positive difference in the lives of their patients.

## Understanding People Who are Ill and Their Families

Quality total care looks at the physical, emotional, spiritual and information needs of the person who is ill and their family members caring for them. Studies show that people who are ill want many of the same things including:

- To be pain free.
- To be alert and aware of what is happening to them.
- To have the companionship of their family and friends.
- To be accepted as the person they have always been.
- To maintain their individuality.
- To not be a burden to their family and caregivers.
- To have familiar things around them: photos, plants, music, flowers, favorite food, pets.
- To be cared for with love and respect.

- To have their family get the support they need to help the person staying at home.
- To have enough information to make informed choices about their treatment and care.

People who are ill and their families must accept responsibility for encouraging improved communication with their professional caregivers because an uncooperative relationship affects the patient and family most directly. This is not always easy because some people have a real fear of anything medical. They may have an uncooperative caregiver or they may have family problems that prevent good communication.

Of course some communication problems between someone who is ill and their professional caregivers come about because the person has few family or friends to support them during discussions with professionals. They may have outlived their spouse or partner, their children may not live nearby or they may be isolated because of a lack of services for our growing number of elders. They can be quite overwhelmed with the well-meaning care of a diverse group of professionals with little support to make sense of their condition, their needs or their personal care at home. These people may fall through the cracks of our health care and home care programs. Extra diligence on the part of professionals within health care facilities and home care programs is necessary to help these people find more natural supports within their communities.

## What Doctors Can Learn From You

There are many things doctors can learn from the person who is ill and from their families:

Facts about the person's condition (this seems obvious but some symptoms are not adequately addressed by the doctor because the person does not talk about new symptoms, there are time constraints or the doctor or person makes assumptions about the condition).

New treatments that you have read about in a popular magazine or seen on a television program that the doctor has not investigated. Sometimes, these treatments are not proven but discussing them can get everyone more involved in treatment decisions. That sense of control improves an ill person's self-image and decreases their anxiety.

People who are ill are always present for every symptom, test, treatment and appointment over the months or years of treatment. They can offer vital feedback on their present treatments, feelings and fears and must never be ignored.

People who are ill must be encouraged by professional caregivers to express their needs and to help the caregivers determine further treatment.

## Some Do's and Don'ts of Improved Communication

From the doctor and other caregivers' points of view there are proven techniques that people can use to improve the patient-caregiver relationship.

### Some Do's

Some people will choose not to try the following suggestions and, in effect, choose not to communicate and cooperate. Whether we agree with their decisions or not, it is their decision and they must be respected unless they injure someone else.

• Know their caregivers' names and help them remember theirs.

- Communicate with them about their physical, emotional, spiritual and information needs.

- Cooperate fully once a decision on treatment is mutually decided.

- Write down the important questions to ask (usually in groups of three) and record the caregiver's answers or bring a loved one along and let them record the answers.

- Respect the caregiver's time while expecting the same in return.

- Ask specific questions rather than, "Why did this happen to me"?

- Offer a time limit for discussion (e.g., 8 minutes) and stick to it. In this way you build up a trusting relationship with the caregivers and they know you respect their time.

## Some Don'ts

Some don'ts include:

- Don't ignore medical instructions after a mutual decision has been made.

- Don't ask too many questions, over and over again. It is better to record the professional's answers.

- Don't bring up questions about other family members and friends in hope of free medical advice.

- Don't keep telephoning with questions to one caregiver that can be better answered by other experts such as a nurse, pharmacist or therapist.

- Don't wait to communicate new pains or negative symptoms until they have become serious.

- Don't forget to communicate emotional and spiritual needs rather than putting on a brave face.

- Don't get a second medical opinion without first telling the principal doctor.

• Don't follow other medical or alternative therapies without consulting the principal doctor because the different therapies may conflict. If your doctor disapproves and you still want to try alternative methods, get another doctor who is more comfortable working in this way.

• Don't forget to treat the caregivers with respect or concern.

## The Differences Between Family Physicians and Specialists

Your *family physician* is responsible for your initial care and diagnosis and for follow-up after treatment by specialists. Some are able to go to the hospital and speak on your behalf with their colleagues and others are not depending on the rules within your health care community.

Your *specialist(s)* are responsible for the diagnosis and treatment of specific illnesses or conditions. When you have more than one condition or illness, you will have several specialists who may, or may not, talk to each other about your care.

Specialists plan your treatment and family physicians help explain and monitor treatment and send you back to specialist(s) for further care, if necessary.

For both types of physicians you will have initial appointments of about 15-30 minutes and then follow-up approximately of about 5-6 minutes. This time is valuable so use it well. You need to write out your questions and concerns and have a family member or friend come with you to write down the answers during the appointment.

Some tips when dealing with specialists:

- Bring a summary of your medical history with you to each appointment, especially what has happened in the last year.
- Bring your drugs with you to every appointment so doctor can verify the drug and dosage and see what other physicians have prescribed since last you met.
- Ask your specialist for either written material or references where you can get more answers to your concerns and questions. For example, if you have recently been diagnosed with diabetes, your specialist cannot explain everything about the condition in a short appointment but can provide you with written material, perhaps even a video or audiotape with common information you will need to know or refer you to a specific patient information clinic. Once you know more about your condition, you can discuss specific concerns not answered in the general information.
- It may be hard to reach your specialist when you are in the middle of treatment. Here are some tips:

If you are in hospital, ask the charge nurse to contact your specialist for you or ask to speak to the physician whose name in on your wristband who is responsible for coordinating your care while you are in the hospital. You may also ask the charge nurse or specialist when they are usually at the hospital so that you can contact them at that time rather than when they have office hours.

If you are at home, ask the nurse/receptionist in the office to have the specialist call you. Many specialists do not mind talking to you once a day during a particularly difficult time for you but more than that is too difficult for them to manage. You should only call them when they are the only person who can help (versus talking with a nurse, home care case manager, social worker, pharmacist, physiotherapist, etc.)

• Have only one family member act as the family's spokesperson so that the physician does not have to give the same answers to each family member. Ideally this person is flexible enough to be at the hospital when the physician has rounds and has a bit of understanding of health care.

• Arrange for a family meeting with the specialist (or specialists if more are involved in the care), responsible nurses and other professionals to deal with unanswered concerns and questions. The hospital social worker may coordinate such a meeting.

• If you have concerns, write them out for the charge nurse or office nurse/receptionist so that the physician can priories their calls. You can imagine that many people want to speak with the specialist so they have to decide who gets called first. They often make their calls at the end of their office hours. Also **leave them the times of day when you are easiest to reach and the telephone number**.

• Some physicians will give out their e-mail address so questions can be answered by e-mail. This is particularly helpful for factual type questions like "When should I be taking these various drugs during the day and do I take them with food or not?"

• It is not helpful to show up to an appointment with a large pile of research you have done at the library or on the Internet. Narrow down your questions and ideas to reasonably fit into the time you have. Many physicians subscribe to their own Internet sources for up-to-date medical information. Ask them to print off relevant sections for you.

• Your specialist does not control the resources of the hospital so their operating room time, the tests that need to be done are not always under their control. The more senior the physician, the more control they have over scheduling.

However, emergencies and unexpected equipment delays or repairs play a large part in who gets what treatment or test and when.

• If your concerns are urgent or you have had difficulty getting hold of your physician, become more assertive and make reasonable demands with deadlines so that the physician understands your urgency. If you cannot be assertive yourself, then ask your family spokesperson to do so. It is a universal truth that people often respond to patients with the greatest need or the loudest demands (the 'squeaky wheel gets the grease'). If you are reasonable and assertive, you will have a better chance of having your concerns and needs met.

## Resolving Communication Problems

When open communication does not seem possible, there are other options available. If the problem has become serious, bring in the community or hospital social worker or the hospital discharge planner or home care case manager to see if improvements can be made. Other caregivers such as a cleric, nurse or psychologist may also be helpful.

When the communication cannot be improved, the person and family can do one or both of the following (although I recognize that during such an emotional time these suggestions will not be easy to follow):

• Change specialists or doctors on the advice of another caregiver.
• Change hospitals or the service you are using.

If there are no alternatives available where you live, ask a family member or friend to become an assertive advocate on your behalf to speak to the caregiver or the organization's president or executive director. The advocate must not stop until they are successful.

If it is the person or family that is uncooperative, the doctor might recommend a different doctor or hospital. She must legally continue care until her patient has found a new doctor.

Many communication problems are not always one person's fault. People have different personalities and for whatever reason, some people do not communicate well with each other. If both people recognize the problem and accept the situation, the caregiver can help find someone to replace him.

In the case of family members, a doctor may find it easier to speak to a single member of the family rather than the whole family. Recognizing that the person is the doctor's most important concern, the family can arrange to choose a member to act as spokesperson and minimize the time a doctor needs to spend with the whole family.

After all the studies have been read, the personal experiences related, and the advice given, the underlying principle of total care of the person who is ill or recovering remains **co-operation between patient, family and caregiver**. A mutual respect and understanding of each others' feelings and needs will result in a fuller life for the person who is ill and a personal satisfaction for the family members and caregivers that they have helped the patient to the best of their abilities.

# Understanding Your Condition

## Questions Doctors Need Answered

You will probably see many doctors, nurses, pharmacists and other caregivers during the length of an illness, medical condition or recovery. They all want some of the same answers to the following questions. If you have written them down in advance, it can save you some time.

- What concerns you about your condition today?
- What is the history of this condition?
- Where in the body did the pain/symptom begin?
- When did it start (date and time)?
- On a scale of 1-10 with 10 equaling the worst pain you have ever had (e.g., broken arm, appendicitis) how do you rate your pain?
- Describe any other symptoms you have had.
- What were you doing at the time of the pain/symptom?
- To what degree does your pain/symptom limit your normal activities?
- How long does the pain/symptom last (an hour, all day)?
- Is the pain/symptom constant or does it change?
- Does the pain/symptom stay in one place or spread out to other parts of your body?
- What makes the pain/symptom worse?
- What makes the pain/symptom better?
- How do the following things affect your symptoms: bowel movements, urination, coughing, sneezing, breathing, swallowing, menstruation, exercise, walking and eating?

- What do you intuitively feel is wrong?
- Do you have any other information that might help me?

## Your Questions about Tests

Even though you are at home now, you may need to return to a hospital or clinic for further tests and treatments. The following questions will help you to understand your condition and have some control over what happens to you. That control will probably help you recover at home faster.

Studies have shown that people who are aware of the physical effects of a test or treatment are less afraid and recover more quickly from a difficult procedure than patients with little or no advanced information. Although caregivers may not have had a particular test themselves, they can usually provide fairly detailed information based on other people's experiences and the medical literature on the specific test or treatment. It is important for a person to understand why a doctor has recommended a test and how the test is done. The following questions can be asked of a doctor, nurse or technician to help the person decide whether or not to consent to the test.

- What is the purpose of this/these tests?
- What do you expect to learn from these tests? Will the results change my treatment in any way?
- What will the test feel like (any pain or discomfort)?
- What are the common risks involved in these tests?
- Are there any after effects of these tests?
- Can my spouse/child/friend come with me? If not, why not? (The medical world is slowly changing to allow someone to be with the patient during difficult tests. The change toward this system is similar to how fathers are now permitted into delivery rooms.)

- Can I return home or to work after the test?
- When will I get the results of these tests? Can I see you to go over them with you?
- What will happen to me if I choose not to take these tests?
- What are the chances of error or false positive/negative results? Some tests have a high incidence of 'false positives'. Often tests cannot be definite but they can help doctors know if they are on the right track.
- What are the costs involved, if any?
- Other questions:

## Your Questions about Medications (Drugs)

You may ask your pharmacist or doctor the following questions. Some information is included with the medication. People are responsible for thinking about these questions whenever they are asked to take new medication. Keep in mind that people react in different ways to medication. Also remember that not following the instructions carefully may lead to poor or even dangerous results.

Some of the answers to the following questions can be found in any of the standard pharmaceutical books listed in the reference section. If your pharmacist or doctor cannot answer your questions with enough detail, check with one of the reference texts.

- What is the name and purpose of these drugs?
- What do the drugs actually do inside my body?
- Will the generic drug absorb in the same way as the name brand drug? If not, do I need a different dosage or different drug?
- How often do I take them each day and for how many days?

- What food, liquids, activities and other medications should I avoid when taking these drugs?
- What are the effects of mixing my various drugs together?
- What are the common and less common side effects of these drugs?
- How can these side effects be controlled?
- If this drug is a narcotic, should I also be getting a stool softener and/or laxative and eating more fibre and drinking more liquids to prevent constipation?
- When should I return to give you feedback about the effectiveness of the drugs? How do I know when I should call you if the drugs produce side effects?
- What will happen if I choose not to take these drugs?
- What are some alternatives to taking drugs for my condition?
- Is there a less expensive generic version of these drugs?
- What special storage instructions should I follow? Pharmacists usually label medication with specific instructions but you should be sure that the labels are present.
- Can this prescription be repeated without coming to see you again?
- What are the costs involved? Many prescriptions are never filled because people do not tell their doctors that they cannot afford the medication.
- Do you know if my medical insurance covers any of these costs? (Ask your insurance agent or government insurance official this question.)
- Other questions:

# Questions to Your Doctors About Your Condition

Once you have been physically examined and appropriate tests are done you will talk with your doctor about your condition. Your family doctor, as your advocate and mediator in the medical world, should help you understand the medical system. Why and how are tests done? What does the diagnosis of your condition mean to you. What treatment alternatives are there? What is the prognosis (prediction of the probable course of a disease) for your condition? What types of support (financial, physical, emotional and spiritual) are available to you?

Try to get your family doctor actively involved if you have trouble understanding or talking with your specialists. Always make sure that you understand what your doctors are saying. It is common for them to use terms you may not understand. Doctors had to learn what these terms meant when they went to school, so they can help you understand them too.

In order not to waste your doctor's time, it is important to ask specific questions. If you know your family doctor well, you might give him a copy of the following checklist of items that you want answered, especially if your situation has changed dramatically since your last visit.

Fill in the answers to your questions (or get a family member or friend to do it for you) so you do not have to repeat the questions at a later point. Also ask for reference material that might answer some of the questions for you. This reduces the time commitment of your doctor and allows you to return later with even more specific questions and concerns. There are times, of course, when your doctor cannot give you specific answers because your disease may not be predictable. However, your doctor can offer some educated guesses with recommendations of where you can go to get further information.

## Diagnosis

Diagnosis is not an exacting science because there are too many unknown variables. This is why second opinions are sometimes necessary. Doctors can usually provide an accurate diagnosis with illnesses and conditions that have exacting scientific tests. One must be careful, however, that the test was done accurately and that the conclusions are confirmed in serious conditions before making major treatment decisions.

- What do I have?
- How did I get it?
- How can I prevent it from happening again or getting worse?
- Other questions:

## The Disease Itself

- Based on your experience and medical studies, what is the usual progress of this disease?
- What can I expect next?
- What other parts of my physical and mental abilities will be affected?
- Other questions:

## Infections

- Can I give this illness to others and if I can, how would they get it from me?
- Other questions:

## Other Possible Diseases

• Could the test results and symptoms indicate a different disease than the one you mention?

• Other questions:

## Treatment

• What treatment do you suggest?

• How does the treatment work?

• How will I evaluate its success or failure?

• How long after I begin the treatment should I see you again to report any progress?

• How often will I need the treatment?

• What are the side effects to this treatment?

• What are some of the medical and non-medical alternatives of these treatments?

• Other questions:

## Prognosis

Prognosis is a prediction of the probable course and outcome of a disease or condition. It is not an exacting science. While you want to know what is probably going to happen to you, there are many variables that may give you a different outcome than what is expected in other people. Your body, mind and spirit are unique and what happens to you may be very different than what happens to other people.

• What is the expected outcome of this illness?

• What will happen if I choose not to treat this illness through medication, surgery or other treatments?

• What are the long-term effects of this illness?

- Will I have pain as the disease develops?
- What is an educated guess to how long I have to live?
- Other questions:

## Questions When You Go to A Hospital

When you go to a hospital, it is important to remember that you are there to receive a service. You remain in control of that service by consenting to, or refusing, the tests and treatments offered to you. You can refuse any and all treatments and tests offered you if you wish, unless you have a communicable disease that may harm others.

- If English is not my first language, is there anyone I can speak to in my own language to help me understand my medical care?

- What is the name of the admitting doctor who I can call if I need help? Who is the doctor in charge of my case and how can I reach them?

- Is the doctor in charge of my case a specialist, intern, resident or medical student?

- What special rules and regulations should I be aware of while I am in this facility?

- What is the discharge procedure for leaving this facility? (You can leave whenever you decide but it may be against a hospital's wishes.)

- Is this a teaching hospital, and if it is, will anyone request that I participate in a research or educational program? (You have the right to consent or refuse to be part of any research or education program.)

- Does the hospital have a patient advocate office or social worker who can answer any of my questions about hospital procedures?

- What costs are involved in my hospital stay, if any?
- Other questions:

# Questions Before Surgery

Surgery is a frightening thing for most people. If people understand the reasons for surgery, the procedures that are followed and the results they can expect, then their fear and anxiety is greatly reduced. Studies have shown that people who understand what is happening to them recover more quickly and often feel less pain because of reduced anxiety.

- What are the benefits and risks to this surgery?
- What are the alternatives, their benefits and risks?
- What is the prognosis if I choose not to have surgery?
- What are the risks of anesthesia in my condition? When will the anesthesiologist meet with me to explain the procedures?
- What is the success rate for this surgery? What is the doctor's own success rate with this surgery?
- What are the pre-surgery procedures?
- What happens during the actual surgery?
- What are the post-surgery procedures?
- Will I have much pain and discomfort after surgery?
- What things can I expect to see so that I am not worried when I wake up, e.g., will I be on a respirator, will I have blood transfusions, and will I be in the intensive care unit?
- What is the expected length for my recovery from surgery?
- How soon after surgery can I go to the bathroom, eat, walk, go home or to work, have sex, smoke and drink alcohol?
- What are the names of the surgeons who will be operating?

- Will there be any medical students operating? (You have the option to refuse treatment by anyone other than your surgeon.)
- What are the costs involved, if any?
- Other questions:

# Creating Your Own Support Team

June Calllwood's book *Twelve Weeks in Spring* tells the story of Margaret Frazer. In 1985 Margaret was dying of cancer and did not want to go into hospital or become involved in a formal palliative care program. June Callwood and other friends recruited close to 60 friends, acquaintances from Margaret's volunteer work, church, and other volunteers to help her stay at home until her death. They provided practical help as well as physical and emotional comforts. Margaret's doctor, Linda Rapson, was part of this 'support team' and provided the others with information to help Margaret stay as comfortable as possible. Near the end of Margaret's life this support team gave round-the-clock care and support.

From that experience several of Margaret's friends from the church of the Holy Trinity and other volunteers established Trinity Home Hospice in Toronto to help people who wanted to keep as much control over their lives as possible through an informal hospice program. The volunteers at Trinity Home Hospice provide practical care and supports during weekly four-hour visits with someone who has a terminal or life-threatening illness. These volunteers are not trained medical staff (although some volunteers have professional backgrounds) nor is their purpose to replace homecare and homemaker supports available through government health care. Their purpose is to provide the kind of practical help and emotional support that friends and good neighbors have provided for each other for generations.

Over the years, several Trinity Home Hospice staff have helped in preparing this information on support circles/teams. Beth Pelton, Elaine Hall, Blair Henry and June Galbraith have been particularly helpful about how people could design their own support teams to allow them the most control and flexibility when they had a terminal or life-threatening illness.

Not everyone wants to receive care through a formal program and others do not have adequate programs available to them. Developing a support team may be one alternative open to such people.

The following ideas are not in any specific order. You might use some or all of the following ideas to develop a support team. Take only those ideas that apply to you and change or add ideas that meet the specific needs of the person getting care. Remember that a support team is only effective when the person agrees with the idea and participates in making decisions.

Keep in mind that the support team idea can be used in many different ways. It can also be used for someone who has a chronic illness; for someone (old or young) living at home alone and needing extra help to stay in their own home; for a parent who wants some time away from the children once or twice a week; and for people who want to increase their circle of friends. In other words, do not be limited by the ideas presented here.

I use the word friends to include family members and friends who do not live with the person, as well as volunteers who over time will probably become friends of the person.

It helps to have one or two friends act as the coordinator(s) of the support team. This person is generally not the spouse or closest loved one. The coordinator is responsible for organizing everyone's schedule for visiting the person. Freeing this responsibility from the closest loved one allows that loved one to concentrate on the person rather than on the day-to-day details of scheduling and answering phone calls. It also gives the person and loved ones more time to relax, go out for walks, eat together quietly, and make plans for themselves and their family.

How do you recruit enough friends? How many do you need? Beth and Elaine suggested that a coordinator ask other friends for their help in visiting the client. As a coordinator (and not the patient or immediate family) people may feel freer to say no if they do not want to participate. In this way there are no hard feelings. People can be recruited from the family, friends and work colleagues who live in the area; people from clubs and organizations that the person belongs to (e.g., service clubs, volunteer work, veterans groups), and where the person worships. Another group that is often overlooked is neighbors. Neighbors are often willing to drop by with some food, help with running errands, cleaning up the outside (e.g., shoveling snow, mowing the lawn), or popping in early in the morning or late at night to help the person with getting up or going to bed. Friends, family and neighbors may also help with basic child care, help people get to appointments, bring someone over to their house for a change of pace and more. The more specific and time-limited the request, the more likely someone will say, "Oh sure. I can do that."

The number of friends one person might need depends completely on the person and family's needs. Some people only want and need the help of a few close people. Other people may need more help, especially near the end of an illness. Trinity Home Hospice often schedules people in the following way if a person needs round-the-clock care – in weekly four-hour shifts. They find that this fits in well with other community supports to ensure seamless, 24-hour care for the person who is ill. The following is a general schedule.

The shifts can actually be slightly longer or shorter depending on the circumstances and needs.

8 a.m. - 12 p.m.

12 p.m. - 4 p.m.

4 p.m. - 8 p.m.

8 p.m. - 8 a.m. (night visit by a friend if possible and necessary)

If a friend wishes to stay overnight, it works best if the friend brings their own linen or sleeping bag and often a change of clothes so that they can leave directly from the person's home to go to work or back to their own home to start the day.

If this schedule is followed it requires four people a day (other than the immediate family that lives with the person) or 28 people a week. Except for the night person, everyone commits to only a four-hour visit once every week. Of course, some people want to participate more often which cuts down on the number of people you need.

It is helpful for everyone on the team to have the monthly schedule and a list of all team members and their telephone numbers. Encourage team members to find their own replacements if they cannot make an appointment and let the coordinator know about any changes to the schedule. Such thoughtfulness can save hours of frustrating telephone calls and communication problems.

As well as visiting the person at home, friends often meet once a month, or more often depending on the need, to compare notes and feelings. Often the person getting care participates in these meetings or they may ask one of their family members to go. These meetings are held in the person's home or elsewhere depending on the person's wishes and the space available.

What qualifications must a friend have? A friend is there to provide emotional support, practical help and companionship and to lessen the fear and isolation of the person and their family. Trinity Home Hospice states some of their qualifications as follows: motivated to help without interfering; emotional maturity; tolerance for different social, cultural and religious beliefs; warmth, empathy, tact and discretion; flexibility; dependability; good listening skills; ability to work with others as a team member; different talents and skills (e.g., from past work experiences and hobbies); and a sense of humor (it is helpful not to take yourself too seriously). The key is to be there for the person and not to fulfill your own, unspoken needs--to provide unconditional support and compassion.

Trinity Home Hospice recommends that clients use the services offered through the Home Care Program and homemaking services where available. These services depend on the area you live in and may include: visits by nurses, physio/occupational therapists, social workers; homemaker help (e.g., to cook some meals, do dishes, do shopping and some light cleaning); and overnight nursing if available.

A logbook is a helpful communication tool when more than a few people are involved in providing support at home. In this log book volunteers, professional caregivers (family doctor, visiting nurses) and family members write notes about the likes and dislikes of the patient and other information that needs to be passed on to different people. The person who is ill often reads the comments and adds comments of her own. Some people who are ill like the idea of a logbook and others do not, so check before hand. The book should also include information about what to do in an emergency, the person's provincial health care number, next of kin, medications, name and number of the coordinator, and name and number of family physician. If for some reason the person needs to go to the hospital the logbook can provide up-to-date information. The book must be kept in a very visible and easy to find place in the house. There should be a checklist of what to do in emergencies and at the time of death and who to call first, second, etc.

People writing in the book should begin with their name, date, time, and length of visit. In point form, you might write the person's activity level (conscious, unconscious); communication ability (recognizing, understanding, speaking coherently or not); eating during the visit; any pain or symptoms; their emotional state or mood (restless, peaceful, worried about....), any activities you did together or discussions you think others would benefit hearing about. Family members can add their own notes about what they heard the doctor or nurse say during their visit.

The logbook is also used to write questions that someone else can answer during a later visit as well as questions you want someone to ask the doctor or nurse during their next visit. There can also be questions or comments to people you know who will visit later such as, "Please make sure that Mom gets the herbal tea rather than the plain one." or "Please check the electric box to see if we need a new fuse for the kitchen," or "Please add the following items to the grocery list." You might also include a 'guest book' portion of the book where guests write in inspirational, spiritual, or funny thoughts or memories of times spent together, etc.

The logbook belongs to the patient and their family. Anyone may read it, so make your writing legible. Do not include confidential information or discussions that others do not need to see. If you include specifics of a conversation, ask the person for permission first.

Recognize that not everyone who wants to help the person will be accepted, for various reasons. If the person prefers not to have someone come to their home, the coordinator tells the person that the person's wishes are paramount and should not be taken personally. Some people do not "click" and that is all right. That person might still participate indirectly by cooking some meals, answering phones, etc.

Recognize that whenever a few people get together there are tensions, misunderstandings and mistakes. People are doing their best but may do little things that annoy each other. Recognize these stresses and discuss them with others on a one-to-one basis or at general meetings if the problem goes beyond a few people. An example is people who enter the person's home without taking off their shoes. This custom is perfectly acceptable in most people's homes but unacceptable in other homes. Knowing these little things help make the experience more positive for everyone. The key is to remember that you are visiting someone's home where they are used to certain routines and behaviors. It is quite different from visiting that person in a hospital where their routines must blend in with the hospital's routines. You are a guest in the home.

It is sometimes difficult to draw the line between giving support and making decisions for the person. Regardless of your views and wishes, you must, as a friend, follow the wishes of the person as best you can. If you strongly disagree with a decision the person has made (on ethical or personal grounds) try to get another friend to be with the person. Call the coordinator to make different arrangements so that you do not have to do something against your strongly held beliefs. At the same time, the person does not have to give up control over their life to make you happy. This line between providing support and making decisions should be discussed at most general meetings to help remind people of this gentle, yet vital, balance.

If the person is ill for a long time there will be friends who come and go because of other commitments. When new people come it is difficult at first for them to fit into what has probably become a tightly knit group. For the person who may be more ill than when the team began, it is one more person coming into their life and home. Recognize some of the difficulties and provide extra support to both the person and new visitor.

Friends hear confidential information from the person who is ill and their family members. All this information is confidential and must not be repeated to anyone without permission. This includes one's own family and curious neighbors. The smaller one's community, the harder it is to keep information confidential. Confidentiality is a useful topic to discuss at a group meeting to ensure the patient's privacy.

Use the talents you have rather than try to learn many new ones. Find people who have the skills and interests you miss so that you can concentrate on giving your talents to the person. For example, you may enjoy reading and writing and can help the person with their mail or read a book with them. Someone else may help without being with the person who is ill. They may enjoy cooking, cleaning, gardening, walking the dog, or running errands without having to spend time with the person. Other people may enjoy helping the person eat their food, doing arts and crafts together, or doing bookkeeping, financial or legal work together (or alone). Still others may enjoy helping the person bathe or go to the bathroom. 'Being there' is also a wonderful gift. Sometimes people don't want to talk, listen or do things. They want to rest, think, pray or daydream. Being there means that you do not interrupt but give the privacy or companionship the person wants.

People who have a cold, flu or infection should not visit the person until they feel better themselves. You do not want to pass on an illness to the person.

At the first meeting of a Trinity Home Hospice Care Team, several key points are highlighted for team members, including:

- Remember that your purpose is to meet the needs of the person you are visiting, not your own needs.
- It is important to remember that the person needs to be able to give as well as receive.
- Continuity of care is very important in functioning teams. We need to act as a team, not a group of individuals. To lessen the disruption to the person and their household, the delivery and standard of care should be as even as possible. We can bring our individuality to the team while acting as a single unit.
- If in your professional life you are a nurse or health care provider, you need to be aware that in this volunteer situation you have a different role to play. Your skills (personal and professional) are an asset to the team but they need to be complimentary to your role as a volunteer.
- A care team requires committed and responsible team members to make it work.

Incorporate this into your life and give it priority in a way that fits in with your other priorities, e.g., family and work.

When you make a commitment, stick to it.

Know your capabilities and respect your limits.

Use others on the team for support.

Confidentiality is critical.

Respect the person's home. It is not just a place of caregiving but their home. This experience is disruptive enough without turning their home into a hospital.

- The coordinator of a team is the focal point for a smooth running team. They act as the center point for information from the person who is ill and all the care providers. This person is the key contact to relieve the burden from the person who is ill and their immediate family. If the team needs to know something quickly, the person only needs to call the coordinator. Team members needing help or advice can look to the team coordinator for this support.

- Care team member roles may include:

Remind the person to take their medication.

Assist with meals.

Be a good listener (non-judgmental and patient).

Understand the difference between being a friend versus a caregiver. As a friend you may challenge your friend about specific issues or concerns; as a caregiver you need to be there as a helper and supporter.

Help to keep the household running smoothly.

Help with taking care of young children.

Help with running errands.

Take the person to appointments.

Respect the privacy of, and give support to, the primary caregiver.

Make sure the person is safe.

Provide care and comfort.

• In the event that you need emergency support while you are on your shift, a list of telephone numbers are supplied to each team member (see the logbook). Remember that you are not alone. You are part of a team; help and support are often just a phone call away.

• To minimize caregiver stress:

Be realistic about your time commitments.

Use the logbook, phone contacts and attendance at meetings to feel supported and improve communication.

Attend training programs in your community that may help now and in the future.

Discuss and deal with your own difficult issues, such as coping with balancing your support with home and work commitments, examining past issues in your relationship with the person, dealing with anger or answering ethical questions.

Be mindful of basic infection control to protect the person who is ill and yourself. Wash your hands thoroughly.

• It is important to keep your commitment to do a shift. Arriving 10 minutes early will enable you to overlap with the previous caregiver. Try to stay 10 minutes longer at the end of your visit. If you need to change your shift, arrange a swap with another team member. Once the swap is arranged, call and have it noted in the logbook at the person's home. Make sure the person and the team coordinator know about the swap. If you cannot arrange a swap, contact the team coordinator for help.

• Unplanned visits, drop-ins and frequent phone calls can make the home environment seem very chaotic. Energy conservation is an important consideration when someone is ill or recovering. If the situation at the home becomes too hectic, suggest scheduling visits from family and friends and encourage people to have shorter visits when necessary.

• Consider specific training in areas where you feel less comfortable. This is especially helpful when assisting someone to move about, transferring them from their bed to a chair, or with personal care. Your local home care organization can give you information on training opportunities.

For more information on care support teams write or call Trinity Home Hospice: 25 King Street West, Commerce Court North, Suite 1102, Box 324, Commerce Court Postal Station, Toronto, Ontario, M5L 1G3. (416) 364-1666. Their web site: www.thh.on.ca/

You may also want to check your phone book to see if you have a local Citizen Advocacy organization in your area. Citizen Advocacy groups have extensive experience helping people who are ill, disabled, vulnerable or marginalized by bringing together community members who want to help others in practical and compassionate ways as friends. According to Cecile Lynes, Co-ordinator of Toronto Citizen Advocacy, "citizen advocates are ordinary community people who are recruited specifically for a person we know who is isolated, marginalized and vulnerable for any number of reasons. Citizen advocates learn by listening to the stories of their vulnerable friends, by walking in their shoes, by experiencing for a time what life is like where their friends live or work or spend time". For more information about Citizen Advocacy, contact the author.

Many disease or condition-specific organizations also provide different kinds of supports (e.g., cancer societies, Red Cross, Meals on Wheels, friendly visiting services, community agencies and private home care agencies). Check your local telephone book or your home care case manager for more information.

# Glossary

*Never be afraid to ask a medical caregiver for the definition of a term. They learned what the word meant when they studied so they can easily explain it to you too.*

The following list includes medical and legal definitions, descriptions of various medical specialists, and common abbreviations used on medical charts and prescriptions. For a complete definition use a more extensive standard medical or legal dictionary.

**abnormal**   Something is not considered 'normal'. For example, a temperature is abnormal if it is below or above the typical level.

**abscess**   A sac of pus formed by the breakdown of infected or inflamed tissue.

**a.c.** abbrev.   Before meals.

**acupressure**   A method of pain relief using finger pressure on the same points used in acupuncture.

**acupuncture**   Chinese medical practice of inserting needles through the skin in specific points to restore the balance of a body's energy flow.

**acute**   Condition with symptoms that develop quickly, are severe, but do not last long. Opposite to chronic condition.

**acute care facility**   Hospitals and medical centers where patients come for relatively quick care for sudden illness, surgery, testing or treatment. Opposite is chronic or long-term care or hospice facilities.

**addiction**   Uncontrollable craving for a substance with an increasing tolerance and physical dependence on it.

**adjuvant treatment**   An added treatment to what is already being done.

**advance directives**   One of two types of legal documents that either give specific instructions or name a substitute decision maker. They may describe what medical treatments a person does, or does not, want under certain circumstances.

**adverse effect**   Negative side effects of a treatment or medication.

**allergist**   A doctor who also specializes in the treatment of allergies.

**allergy** A reaction substances that may cause a rash, swelling or more serious physical response.

**alopecia** Temporary or permanent loss of hair (may occur as a side effect of chemotherapy).

**ambulatory** The ability of someone to walk. Ambulatory centers refer to health care facilities where people go for part of a day for treatment.

**amyotrophic lateral sclerosis (ALS)** A deterioration of the spinal cord that results in the wasting away of muscles. Also called Lou Gerhig's Disease.

**analgesic** A pain-relieving drug.

**anaphylaxis** An exaggerated, often serious, allergic reaction to proteins and other substances.

**anemia** A decrease in red blood cells or in the hemoglobin content of the red corpuscles. The normal count is 4.0 to 6.0 $\times 10^{12}$.

**anesthesia** Total or partial loss of sensation from an injection, ingestion or inhalation of a drug. General anesthetics put a patient to sleep for a short time. Local anesthetics numb an area of your body without putting you to sleep (e.g., dentist's anesthetic for a tooth filling).

**anesthesiologist** A doctor specializing in providing an anesthetic during surgery and monitoring the patient's vital signs.

**aneurysm** A swollen or distended area in a blood vessel wall.

**angina** The pain that results from not enough blood going to the heart.

**angiogram** X-ray studies in which a dye is injected into the bloodstream to detect abnormalities in blood vessels, tissues and organs.

**anorexia** The loss of appetite experienced by most people near the end of their lives.

**antacid** A substance that neutralizes acid.

**antibiotic** Drugs that check the growth of bacteria but do not work against viruses.

**antibody** A substance produced in our bodies to fight against bacteria.

**anticonvulsant** A medication used to prevent seizures.

**antitussive** A drug used to relieve coughing.

**apnea** Extended periods when breathing stops during sleep.

**apoplexy** (*See* **stroke**)

**arrhythmia** An abnormal heartbeat.

**aspiration** Fluid that gets into the lungs.

**asthma** A tightening of the air passages that leads to wheezing and difficult breathing.

**assets** All of a person's properties, including real estate, cash, stocks and bonds, art, furniture etc., and claims against other people (e.g., loans).

**asymptomatic** Someone without any symptoms.

**atrophy** A wasting or withering away of part of the body.

**autopsy** An examination of a dead body to determine the cause of death; the post-mortem ordered by the coroner or medical examiner.

**barbiturate** A type of sleeping pill.

**barium enema** Radiopaque barium (visible by x-ray) is put into the lower bowel (colon) and rectum by an enema for an x-ray. Also called a Lower GI Series.

**bedsore** A sore that develops when pressure causes inadequate blood circulation to the skin. For persons confined to bed, good skin care, repositioning, cushioning and some limited activity are the best treatment. Also called decubitus ulcers.

**beneficiary** Person who receives a benefit from a will, insurance policy or trust fund.

**benign** Non-malignant self-limiting condition that is not life threatening.

**b.i.d.** abbrev. Twice a day.

**biopsy** An examination of body tissue with a microscope to help in diagnosis. Tissue is removed from the body by surgery, insertion of a needle into tissue and other methods.

**blood gas test** A blood test to determine the level of oxygen and carbon dioxide in the blood.

**blood pressure** Measures the force of the blood coming from the heart against the walls of the blood vessels. (See *hypertension*) The measurement is recorded as two numbers; e.g., 130/80.

**bolus**  An amount given all at once.

**bone marrow test**  A needle is inserted into a bone (hipbone or breastbone) to remove a sample of bone marrow for diagnostic purposes e.g., to diagnose leukemia, aplastic anemia.

**brain scan**  Also called carotid angiogram. A radioactive substance is injected into a neck artery for a brain x-ray using a scanning camera.

**CAT (or CT) Scan**  A computerized axial tomography scan. X-rays of the body or head are taken using a computer to give a slice-by-slice view of the area.

**CCU (Coronary Care Unit)**  Unit in a hospital which provides intensive care to heart patients.

**cancer**  A malignant tumor that tends to invade healthy tissue and spread to new sites.

**candidiasis**  A fungal infection known as 'thrush' in one's mouth, throat, esophagus or other dark, moist areas (e.g., vagina).

**carbohydrates**  Best source of energy for your body. Found in most foods but especially sugars and starches. If you eat too much, however, your body changes and stores them as fats.

**carcinogenic**  Something that can cause cancer.

**cardiac**  Refers to the heart.

**cardiac surgeon**  Doctors specializing in heart surgery.

**cardiologist**  Doctor specializing in the diagnosis and treatment of heart conditions.

**cardiovascular surgeon**  Doctor specializing in surgery of blood vessels of the heart.

**caregivers**  Include professional health care providers and volunteers. **Primary caregiver** is usually a family member or close friend who provides most of the physical care for a person at home (e.g., wife, husband, lover, best friend).

**catheter**  A plastic or rubber tube that puts in or takes out fluids from your body. A common example is a bladder catheter (Foley) to allow urine to leave the bladder freely.

**c.c.** abbrev.  Cubic centimeter; also can mean with meals or food.

**cerebral palsy**  Impaired muscular power and coordination from failure of nerve cells in the brain.

**chemotherapy**  Drug therapy against infection or cancer that can destroy bacteria or dangerous cells.

**cheyne-stoking**  A pattern of breathing where the respiration rates increase and then decrease followed by increasing periods of not breathing.

**chiropractor**  Doctors without a medical degree specializing in manipulation of the spine; cannot prescribe medication or perform surgery.

**chronic**  A prolonged or lingering condition.

**clinical nurse specialist (CNS)**  A registered nurse with a Master's Degree in Nursing who specializes in one aspect of health care and is involved in research and teaching.

**codicil**  An appendix or supplement to a will (e.g., to change the name of your beneficiary).

**colostomy**  A surgical opening from the body surface (usually through the abdomen) into the colon which acts as an artificial anus. Colostomy bags collect the body's waste. Depending on a patient's condition a colostomy may be temporary or permanent.

**coma**  A deep, prolonged unconsciousness.

**competence**  Legal competence to make decisions for one's self is difficult to determine because incompetence may not be permanent and definitions of legal competence depends on where one lives.

**complementary therapies**  Includes therapies like: acupuncture, aroma therapy, art, autosuggestion, biofeedback, chiropractic, herbal, homeopathy, music, naturopathy, osteopathy and therapeutic touch.

**congenital**  Something present since birth.

**COLD (Chronic Obstructive Lung Disease)**  (*See* **COPD**)

**conjunctivitis**  A redness and irritation of the thin membrane that covers the eye.

**COPD (Chronic Obstructive Pulmonary Disease)**  Includes illnesses like emphysema. Also called COLD for chronic obstructive lung disease.

**coronary**  Refers to the blood vessels that supply the heart.

**CPR**  Cardiopulmonary resuscitation is used on patients who are not breathing and have no pulse. Trained professionals or volunteers use artificial respiration (mouth-to-mouth breathing) and manually pump the patient's heart by compressing the chest with their hands to simulate a regular pulse.

**culture**  A test for infection or organisms that could cause infection.

**CVA (Cerebrovascular accident)**  Also called a stroke.

**cystoscopy**  A long flexible tube, attached to a miniature camera, is passed through the urinary tract into the bladder.

**d.** abbrev.  Give.

**dd. in d** abbrev.  From day to day.

**dec** abbrev.  Pour off.

**decubitus ulcer**  (*See* **bedsore**)

**dehydrated**  Lack of moisture in the body.

**dementia**  Deterioration of a person's mental capacity from changes in the brain.

**depressant**  A drug to reduce mental or physical activity.

**dermatologist**  Doctor specializing in skin conditions.

**diagnosis (dx)**  An analysis of someone's physical and/or mental condition.

**diastolic**  The lower number in the blood pressure reading. Refers to the resting phase of a heartbeat.

**dil** abbrev.  Dilute.

**disp.** abbrev.  Dispense.

**diuretic**  A drug to increase urine output, relieving edema or swelling.

**do not resuscitate (DNR)**  A written order that the doctor makes, usually with the patient-family's consent, not to resuscitate the person if they have a cardiac or respiratory arrest. This is usually written near the end of someone's life so that no CPR or treatments are done to prolong the person's life.

**doctor**  Common title for a doctor.

**doppler** Sound waves. Also the name for a test that can detect a deep vein thrombosis (DVT).

**dos** abbrev. Dose.

**draw sheet** A folded bed sheet placed sideways on the bed under a patient. Two people on either side of the bed can then lift the draw sheet and the patient to move them up or down in bed or to help them turn the person onto their side or back.

**dur dolor** abbrev. While pain lasts.

**Dx** abbrev. Diagnosis.

**dysphagia** Difficulty in swallowing.

**dysplasia** Abnormal cells.

**dyspnea** Shortness of breath.

**ECG** (*See* **EKG**)

**echocardiogram** Sound wave test of the heart.

**EKG (Electrocardiogram)** A record of the electrical current produced by the heart. Diagnoses abnormal cardiac rhythm and damage to the muscle of the heart. Also ECG.

**EEG (Electroencephalogram)** A record of the electrical current produced by the brain.

**edema** Excess collection of fluid in the tissues.

**electrolyte imbalance** When salts or chemicals in the blood are not balanced correctly.

**embolism** Blockage of a blood artery by a clot. In the brain it can cause a stroke.

**EMG (Electromyography)** Test to evaluate the electrical activity of nerves and muscles.

**emesis** Vomiting.

**emp** abbrev. As directed.

**empiric** Based on experience.

**emphysema** A condition of the lungs with labored breathing and increased risk of infection. The lungs lose their elasticity and function.

**endocrinologist** A specialist in diagnosing and treating disorders of the endocrine glands (glands affecting hormones) and their secretions.

**endoscopic exam** Using a thin, lighted tube to examine an internal part of the body.

**enema** A fluid injected into the rectum to clean out the bowel or to give drugs.

**enteral** Something given by way of the intestines.

**epidural anesthesia** Medication given through a thin tube into your spine. Common in woman having babies as it allows the mother to be alert with pain relief.

**estate** All of one's assets and liabilities, especially those left by a deceased.

**executor** The person named in a will to dispose of the assets and pay, from estate funds, the liabilities of a deceased.

**executrix** The female noun for executor.

**family** Includes people who are part of one's immediate family and those we define as members of our family through friendship and love. In legal terms, each province and state has different definitions that may restrict family members to biologically related members.

**family practitioner** Doctor who diagnoses and treats the general illnesses and problems of patients and refers them to a specialist when necessary.

**febris** Latin for *fever*.

**feces** Waste product resulting from a bowel movement.

**fibrillation** Irregular heart beat or an involuntary muscle contraction.

**gastroenterologist** Doctor specializing in the digestive system: esophagus, stomach and bowels.

**geneticist** Specialist in genetic diseases - hereditary disorders and abnormalities.

**geriatrician (gerontologist)** Specialist in the diagnoses and treatment of illnesses in older people.

**GI (Gastrointestinal) Series** An x-ray examination of the esophagus, stomach, colon and rectum.

**GI Series-Lower** (*See* **barium enema**)

**gm.** abbrev. Grams.

**gr.** abbrev. Grains.

**gtt.** abbrev. Drops.

**h** abbrev. Hour.

**hallucination** The feeling of seeing or hearing something that is not there.

**hematologist** Doctor specializing in conditions of the blood.

**hematoma** Swelling caused by bleeding into tissues as in a bruise.

**hemiplegia** One-sided paralysis of the body, usually from a stroke. A right-sided paralysis indicates left-sided brain damage.

**hemoglobin** The protein in red blood cells that carry oxygen to the body tissues. The normal count is 12-18 g/dL.

**hemorrhage** Extensive abnormal bleeding.

**heparin lock** A needle is placed in the arm with blood thinner to keep the blood from clotting inside the needle or tubing.

**hepatoma** Cancer or tumor of the liver.

**hereditary** Something inherited from parents.

**high blood pressure** (*See* **hypertension**)

**Hodgkin's disease** A form of lymphoid cancer that has high fever, enlarged lymph nodes and spleen, liver and kidneys and a dangerously lowered resistance to infection.

**hormone** A glandular excretion into the blood that stimulates another organ.

**hospice** (*See* **palliative care**) Also name for a free-standing institution where palliative care is given to people with a terminal illness. Programs often have major home care component and may also be part of an established institution such as a hospital.

**h.s.** abbrev. At bedtime, before retiring. From the Latin *hora somni.*

**Huntington's chorea** A hereditary condition with symptoms of uncontrolled movements and progressive mental disorder.

**hypercalcemia/hypocalcemia** Too high (more than 10.5 mg/dL), or too low (less than 8.8 mg/dL), calcium level in the blood.

**hyperkalemia/hypokalemia** Too high (more than 5.0 mEq/L), or too low(less than 3.8 mEq/L), potassium level in the blood.

**hypernatremia/hyopnatremia** Too high(more than 145 mEq/L), or too low(less than 136 mEq/L), sodium (salt) level in the blood.

**hypertension** High blood pressure. The systolic number (the top one) is usually above 140mmHg and the diastolic number (the lower one) is usually above 90 mmHg. Can lead to a stroke, heart failure or other serious condition if not treated. The pressure measures the force of the blood expelled from the heart against the walls of the blood vessels.

**hypnotic** A drug used to induce sleep.

**hypnotism** A treatment that puts a patient into a sleep-like trance to enhance memory or make the person susceptible to suggestion. Can be used in pain relief and to eliminate some negative habits.

**hypotension** Low arterial blood pressure.

**hypoxia** Low oxygen level in the blood.

**I&O** abbrev. Intake and output refers to fluids into and out of body.

**iatrogenic disease** A condition caused by a doctor or a hospital stay.

**ICU (Intensive Care Unit)** Unit within a hospital where seriously ill or post-operative patients receive intensive care.

**incontinence** Lack of bladder or rectal control

**in d** abbrev. Daily. From the Latin *in dies*.

**idiopathic** Unknown cause.

**infarct** Death of tissue because of lack of blood supply.

**infarction** Blockage of a blood vessel especially the artery leading to the heart.

**infection** Inflammation or disease caused when bacteria, viruses and other microorganisms invade the body.

**infectious disease** Disease which is passed from one person to another person.

**inflammation** Swelling or irritation of tissue.

**insomnia** An inability to sleep.

**intern** A recent medical school graduate undergoing supervised practical training.

**internist** Doctor who specializes in the nonsurgical treatment of the internal organs of the body.

**intramuscular** Something (e.g., medication) given into a muscle. (*See* **blood pressure**)

**IV** abbrev. Intravenous in which a needle is kept within a vein for the injection of medication or blood.

**intraperitoneal** Into the abdominal cavity.

**intubate** Putting a tube into a person's airway to help them breathe.

**invasive procedure** Anything that punctures, opens or cuts the skin.

**laxative** A drug that causes bowel movements.

**lethargy** Sleepiness.

**leukemia** Cancer of white blood cells in which these cells reproduce abnormally.

**liabilities** Debts owed to others such as a loan, mortgage, utility bills, credit card payments, etc.

**life-sustaining procedures** These may include artificial means of keeping someone hydrated and fed, CPR, blood transfusions and mechanical ventilation.

**life-threatening illness** Any condition or disease that can lead to sudden or quicker-than-expected death.

**lipid** Fat.

**living will** A form of advance directives that lists what life-sustaining treatments the person does, or does not, want in situations listed in the document.

**lumbar puncture** A diagnostic procedure in which a hollow needle is inserted between two lumbar vertebrae in the spinal cord to remove some spinal fluid.

**lymph glands** Nodes of tissue that provide a system of protection against bacteria and other attacks against the body's immune system.

**m et n** abbrev. Morning and night.

**malaise**  A vague feeling of discomfort; feeling bad.

**malignant**  Progressive or terminal condition.

**malnutrition**  Insufficient consumption of essential food elements whether by improper diet or illness.

**mammography**  An x-ray of the breasts to detect tumors.

**meningitis**  Inflammation of the membranes covering and protecting the brain and spinal cord.

**metastasis**  The spreading of an infection or cancer from the original area to others in the body.

**mg.** abbrev.  Milligrams.

**MI** abbrev.  Myocardial infarction; a heart attack.

**mor dict** abbrev.  In the manner directed.

**morbidity**  Serious disease; an undesired result or complication.

**mortality**  Death or death rate.

**mobility**  The ability to move.

**MRI** abbrev.  Magnetic resonance imaging; a picture of the body that uses magnetic energy rather than x-ray energy.

**multiple sclerosis**  A degenerative disease of the central nervous system where parts of the brain and spinal cord harden.

**muscular dystrophy**  A degenerative muscle disease in which muscles waste away.

**myalgia**  Muscle aches.

**nasogastric tube**  A tube from the nose to the stomach to give nutrition and medication.

**neoplasm**  A tumor or a new growth of abnormal tissue where cells multiply. (*See* **cancer**).

**nephrologist**  Doctor specializing in kidney conditions.

**neurologist**  Doctor specializing in the nervous system.

**neurosurgeon**  Doctor specializing in surgery of the nervous system.

**non rep** abbrev.  Do not repeat.

**nosocomial pneumonia** Pneumonia acquired in the hospital.

**notarize** A notary public authenticates or attests to the truth of a document (e.g., attests that a document was signed by a particular person).

**notary public** A public officer (can be a lawyer) who certifies documents, takes affidavits and administers oaths.

**nurse practitioner** Registered Nurse who has received additional training in order to perform more specialized care than other nurses.

**o** abbrev. None.

**obstetrician/gynecologist** Doctor specializing in conditions of the female reproductive system. Obstetricians specialize in pregnancies and births.

**occlusion** Closing or an obstruction.

**oncology** The study of tumors or cancer.

**oncologist** Doctor specializing in tumors and cancer.

**ophthalmologist** Doctor who specializes in diseases of the eye.

**opioids** These drugs come from opium. They are generally used to relive severe pain. Heroin, methadone and morphine all come from the opium plant.

**optician** Non-doctor trained in filling prescriptions for eyeglasses and contact lenses.

**optometrist** Non-doctor trained to measure vision and make eyeglasses and contact lenses.

**orthopedist** Doctor specializing in bones.

**osteopathy** Diagnosis and treatment of disorders by manipulative therapy, drugs, surgery, proper diet and psychotherapy.

**osteoporosis** The bones become weaker because of a loss of calcium.

**otolaryngologist** A specialist in conditions of the ear, throat and nose.

**palliative care** Treatment to relieve symptoms, rather than cure, a disease or condition. Includes meeting the physical, emotional, spiritual and information needs of patients. Also called hospice care.

**paracentesis** Fluid drainage by inserting a tube into the body.

**parenteral**  Administration of medication or nutrition into the body by injections.

**Parkinson's disease**  A progressive nervous disease. Symptoms are muscular tremor, slowing of movement, partial facial paralysis and impaired motor control.

**pathogenesis**  The initial cause of a disease.

**pathologist**  Doctor who examines tissue and bone to diagnose if there is a malignancy. They also perform autopsies.

**pathology**  The scientific study of disease.

**patient**  Someone who receives treatment. Sometimes called client, consumer or customer.

**pc** abbrev.  After meals.

**pediatrician**  Doctor specializing in the care of children.

**per os (po)** abbrev.  By mouth.

**percutaneous**  Through the skin.

**pH test**  Determines the degree of acidity or alkalinity in the urine.

**pharmacokinetics**  Study of how the body absorbs, distributes and gets rids of a drug.

**phlebitis**  Irritation or inflammation of a vein.

**physiatrist**  Doctor specializing in rehabilitative therapy after illness or injury.

**physician**  A medical doctor as opposed to doctors with a Ph.D.

**placebo**  A substance containing no medication. It can help a patient who believes that it will work. A practical and effective treatment for some people.

**plasma**  The liquid part of blood (55% of total volume).

**plastic surgeon**  Doctor specializing in reconstructive and cosmetic surgery.

**platelets**  Small particles in the blood that help with blood clotting.

**pneumonia**  An acute or chronic disease which inflames the lungs and fills them with fluid.

**p.o.** abbrev.  By mouth. From the Latin *per os.*

**podiatrist** Non-doctor who specializes in the care, treatment and surgery of feet.

**powers of attorney** There are two main types of legal powers of attorney documents that a person signs to delegate legal decision making to one or two people of their choice. The first gives someone *financial and legal decision-making power* from the time the document is signed until the document is revoked by the patient, and the second gives all *health care related decisions* away **only if the patient cannot speak for themselves at the time**. It is advisable to separate the two types of documents so that one person is not responsible for all decisions and not in a conflict of interest.

**primary caregiver** (*See* **caregiver**)

**prn** abbrev.  Give as needed, as often as necessary.

**proctologist** Doctor specializing in diagnoses and treatment of disorders and diseases of the anus, colon and rectum.

**prognosis (Px)** A prediction of the future course of a condition or illness based on scientific study. It is only a prediction and should not be accepted as fact.

**prophylaxis** A drug given to prevent disease or infection.

**prosthesis** An artificial substitute for a part of the body such as an arm or leg.

**protocol** A plan of study.

**psychiatrist** Doctor who specializes in the diagnosis and treatment of emotional and medical disorders.

**psychologist** A professional with a Ph.D. in psychology who diagnoses and treats psychological disorders. They may not prescribe medication.

**pt** abbrev.  Patient.

**pulmonary** Refers to the lungs.

**Px** abbrev.  Prognosis.

**q** abbrev.  Every.

**q.d.** abbrev.  Every day; daily.

**q.h.** abbrev.  Every hour. From the Latin *quaque hora.*

**q.i.d.** abbrev. Four times a day. From the Latin *quater in die*.

**qn** abbrev. Every night. From the Latin *quaque nox*.

**qod** abbrev. Every other day.

**qs** abbrev. Proper amount, quantity sufficient.

**quack** Opportunist who uses questionable or worthless methods or devices in diagnosing and treating various diseases.

**ql** abbrev. As much as desired. From the Latin *quantum libet*.

**radiation therapy** X-ray or cobalt treatment.

**radiologist** Doctor who interprets X-rays. Sub-specialties include nuclear medicine and angiography.

**radiology** A branch of science using radiant energy, as in x-rays, especially in the diagnosis and treatment of disease.

**recombinant** New combinations of genes.

**refractory** Not responding to treatment.

**regimen** A program or set of rules to follow for treatment of a condition.

**relapse** The return or reappearance of a disease.

**remission** Disappearance of evidence of cancer or other diseases.

**renal** Refers to the kidneys.

**rep** abbrev. Repeat.

**resect** Remove or cut out surgically.

**resident** Doctor receiving specialized clinical training.

**respirologist** Specialist who diagnoses and treats diseases of the lungs and respiratory (breathing) system.

**respite care** Time away for rest. This might mean that a family caregiver goes away for a few days or that the person who is ill goes to a hospice program.

**rheumatologist** Specialist who diagnoses and treats rheumatic diseases that cause by inflammation or pain in the joints and muscles.

**Rx** abbrev. Prescription or therapy.

**satiety (early)** Feeling full or bloated quickly after eating very little food.

**sedative**  A medication to calm a person or make them less anxious.

**senility**  Loss of mental ability and memory (especially of recent events).

**shiatsu**  (*See* **acupressure**)

**shock**  Sudden, acute failure of the body's circulatory function.

**sig** abbrev.  Write, let it be imprinted.

**somnolence**  Sleepiness.

**spinal tap**  (*See* **lumbar puncture**)

**standard of care**  A treatment plan which the majority of health care providers accept as appropriate.

**stat** abbrev.  Right away. From the Latin *statim.*

**stomatitis**  Mouth sores or inflammation of the mouth.

**stroke**  Sudden loss of muscular control, sensation and consciousness caused by the rupture or blocking of a blood vessel in the brain.

**subclavian**  Under the collarbone.

**subcutaneous**  Often refers to medication placed under the skin by a needle.

**sublingual**  Often refers to medication placed under the tongue.

**substitute decision maker**  This person is chosen by a patient in an advance directive document to make decisions about health care and treatment when a patient cannot speak for themselves.

**supine**  Lying on the back.

**supportive care**  General medical care that treats symptoms; not intended to improve or cure the underlying disease or condition. Sometimes called palliative care although not limited to people with a terminal or life-threatening illness.

**suppository**  A medication given in solid form and inserted into the rectum or vagina. Dissolves into a liquid by body heat.

**surgeon**  Doctor who treats a disease by surgery. Surgeons generally specialize in one or more types of surgery.

**symptom**  An indication of a certain condition or disease.

**symptomatic**  Having symptoms.

**syndrome** A group of symptoms that indicate a specific disease or condition.

**systolic** Top number in blood pressure; refers to the contraction phase of a heart beat.

**TENS** Trans-cutaneous electrical nerve stimulation. A device that provides mild amounts of electrical stimulus to different parts of the body as a way to reduce pain.

**temperature** Normal oral temperature is 97-99° Fahrenheit or 36-37.2° Celsius. Changes +/- one degree during the day.

**terminal illness** Often classified as any illness that will lead to death soon. The length of time used is often between 3-12 months.

**thoracic surgeon** Doctor who specializes in chest surgery.

**thrombosis** Blood clotting within blood vessels.

**t.i.d.** abbrev. Three times a day. From the Latin *tres in die.*

**titration** Gradual change in drug dose to determine the best effect or dose of a drug.

**tolerance** Drug tolerance is when there is increased resistance to the usual effect of a drug as a result of long-term use.

**topical** On the skin or surface.

**toxicity** Side effects or undesirable effects of a drug.

**toxin** A poison or harmful agent.

**transdermal** Through the skin.

**trauma** An injury or wound.

**tumor** (*See* **neoplasm**)

**Tx** abbrev. Treatment.

**ultrasound scan** A picture of internal organs using high frequency sound waves.

**urine** Liquid released when bladder empties.

**urologist** Doctors specializing in urinary tract and male prostate gland diseases plus male sexual dysfunction.

**ut dict** abbrev. As directed.

**vascular surgeon**  Doctor specializing in blood vessel surgery.

**venipuncture**  Going into a vein with a needle.

**vital signs**  Measurement of temperature, pulse, respiration rate and blood pressure.

**vomiting**  A reflex action that contracts the stomach and ejects the contents through the mouth.

**x-ray**  Electromagnetic radiation used to create pictures of the body's internal structures.

**x-ray dye**  A substance injected into a vein before an X-ray to highlight an area for examination. May cause an allergic reaction.

**WBC**  White blood cells that fight infection. The normal count is 5,000 to 10,000.

# References

The following is a selection of recommended books. Some were used to research and prepare this book. They certainly do not include all the books available on the various subjects in this book. *My first recommendation is that you check your local bookstore and library for the most recent and up-to-date books on the topic you are most interested in.*

When checking any source for health care information, expect to find information that might be unsettling. The information may tell you things you didn't expect or didn't want to know and it may be written for a professional audience rather than for patients and families.

Some of the books in this reference list may have more recent, up-dated editions. If a particular author interests you, check the library for their other books.

The companion book to this one is *Family Hospice Care*, which lists references more specific to hospice care.

## Books

Appearance Concepts Foundation of Canada. (1990). *Changes, choices and challenges.* Toronto: Appearance Concepts Foundation of Canada. This book gives practical information on using scarves and wigs to cover one's head as well as information on skin care for women who have had radiation or chemotherapy.

Berman, Claire. (1995). *Caring for yourself while caring for your aging parents: How to help, how to survive.* New York: Henry Holt. This book discusses the stresses and needs of caregivers.

Callwood, June. (1986). *Twelve weeks in spring.* Toronto: Lester and Orpen Dennys. The story of how 60 friends and colleagues took care of Margaret Frazer in her own home.

First Aid Books: Any first aid book (and course) to help keep you up-to-date on emergency procedures, CPR and mouth-to-mouth resuscitation such as those by the Canadian Association of Emergency Physicians, Red Cross, St. John's Ambulance or YMCA.

Haller, James. (1994). *What to eat when you don't feel like eating.* Hantsport, Nova Scotia: Robert Pope Foundation. A cookbook for people preparing food for others who are suffering a serious illness.

Larson, David E. (Ed.). (1996). *Mayo Clinic family health book.* (2nd ed.). New York: William Morrow. Extensive illustrated home medical reference including diagnosis, prevention, treatment alternatives and more.

Mace, Nancy L. and Rabins, Peter V. (1999). *The 36-hour day: A family guide to caring for persons with Alzheimer's Disease, related dementing illnesses and memory loss in later life.* (3rd ed.). Baltimore, MD: Johns Hopkins Press. A text for families caring for loved ones.

McLeod, Beth W. (1999). *Caregiving: The spiritual journey of love, loss, and renewal.* Etobicoke, ON: Wiley.

Neal, Margaret B and Chapman, Arthur C. (1993). *Balancing work and caregiving: For children, adults and elders.* Thousand Oaks, CA: Sage.

Perry, Anne Griffin. (1998). *Pocket guide to basic skills and procedures.* New York: Mosby Year Book. More complete information on all the techniques suggested in this book from a nurse's perspective.

Silverman, Harold. (Ed.). (1998). *The pill book: The illustrated guide to the most prescribed drugs in the United States.* (8th ed.). New York: Bantam Doubleday Dell.

van Bommel, Harry. (2002). *Family hospice care.* Toronto: Resources Supporting Family and Community Legacies Inc. Written to help family and friends take care of people at home who are dying.

# The Internet

The following Internet links may be helpful to those of you interested in more information about home care. I have picked just a few sites that have excellent resources and extensive links to other related sites.

**A note of caution**: There are thousands of web sites offering health care information. The information on some sites may not be accurate or current. Check to see who produces the web site, their qualifications and their credibility before assuming their information is correct.

Also, when checking the web, or another other source, for health care information, expect to find information that might be unsettling. The information may tell you things you didn't expect or didn't want to know and it may be written for a professional audience rather than for patients and families.

For general and advanced health information, good starting points include:

**Caregiver Network Inc.**
www.caregiver.on.ca
Developed for people who are caring for elderly family members and friends.

**Dr. Koop's Community**
www.drkoop.com
An interactive health site with daily updates and news.

## Health Canada's Information Site
www.hc-sc.gc.ca
An extensive site with many links to other reputable sites.

## Canadian Health Network
www.canadian-health-network.ca
A general health information site with links to many other health related sites.

## Mayo Clinic.Com
www.mayoclinic.com
An outstanding site for general health information

## UpToDate
www.uptodate.com
A clinical reference for physicians who subscribe but also includes patient information that is updated regularly.

# Finding Out About Local Home And Health Care Programs

Home care is a group of services to help people live at home when they are ill or recovering from an illness or surgery rather than staying in a hospital or long-term care facility.

## Basic Services

- Visiting nurses
- Home support (help with homemaking such as light housekeeping, shopping, cooking, laundry)
- Physiotherapy
- Occupational therapy
- Respiratory therapy
- Social work counseling
- Nutritional counseling
- Housing registry
- Personal emergency response systems

## Complex Services

- Home intravenous antibiotic therapy
- Life support/ventilator assistance systems
- Services for children with complex needs
- Tube feedings (either by nose or through the stomach wall)
- Home cancer therapy
- Palliative or hospice care
- Care for people who have some form of dementia.

# Community Support Services

- Adult day centers
- Meals-on-wheels and/or wheels to meals programs
- Respite care (so that caregivers can have some time off)
- Transportation help
- Help with shopping
- Help with home maintenance.

Home care programs across Canada and the United States provide different services. To find out what is available in your community, you can check with your family doctor, community health office, or other home health care providers. If a particular service is not available in your community, ask your political leaders why and how your community can arrange to get such service in the near future. If you have difficulty in finding out what services are available, you can contact:

**Canadian Home Care Association**
(613) 569-1585
www.cdnhomecare.on.ca

**National Association for Home Care**
(202) 547-7424
www.nahc.org

**Respite** care may be available in your community to provide extra support so that family caregivers can take a short break. Check with your local home care, hospice or long-term care groups.

The following organizations have many services and information to offer. Check your telephone book for local offices or check with the national office or web sites.

If you are getting information by phone, always have a list of questions written out and write any answers on the same sheet of paper including the name of the person you spoke to.

## Hospice Palliative Care

To locate hospice and palliative care programs, check your telephone directory or these national organizations:

**Canadian Hospice Palliative Care Association**
1 (800) 668-2785
www.cpca.net

**National Hospice Palliative Care Organization**
(703) 887-1500
www.nhpco.org

# Health Care Organizations

If you live outside of an urban center, you can call Area Code + 555-1212 to get the branch office in the city nearest you. If you have access to the Internet, use www.yahoo.com or www.canada411.ca to help you locate services nearest to you.

**AIDS Committees**
Check your local telephone directory or nearest urban center.

**Alzheimer Society of Canada (and related Dementias)**
1 (800) 616 8816
www.alzheimer.ca

**Amyotrophic Lateral Sclerosis (ALS) Society of Canada**
1 (800) 267-4257
www.als.ca

**Arthritis Society**
1 (800) 321-1433
www.arthritis.ca

**Bereavement support services (grief counseling)**
Check your telephone directory.

**Brain Tumor Foundation**
1 (800) 265 5106
www.btfc.org

**Canadian Association of Retired Persons**
1 (800) 363 9736
www.fifty-plus.net

**Canadian Cancer Society (Cancer Information Services)**
1 (888) 939 3333
www.cancer.ca

**Canadian Continence Foundation (incontinence)**
1 (800) 265 9575
www.continence-fdn.ca

**Canadian Diabetes Association**
1 (800) 226 8464
www.diabetes.ca

**Canadian Hemophilia
Society**
1 (800) 668 2686
www.hemophilia.ca

**Canadian Lung
Association**
1 (888) 566-LUNG
www.lung.ca

**Canadian Medic Alert
Foundation**
1 (800) 668 1507
www.medicalert.ca

**Canadian Red Cross
Society**
1 (800) 418 1111
www.redcross.ca

**Childhood Cancer
Foundation –
Candlelighters Canada**
1 (800) 363 1062
www.candlelighters.ca

**Distress Lines**
Check your local telephone
book on the inside cover.

**Epilepsy Canada**
1 (800) 860 5499
www.epilepsy.ca

**The Heart and Stroke
Foundation of Canada**
1 (888) 473 4636
www.heartandstroke.ca

**Kidney Foundation of
Canada**
1 (800) 361 7494
www.kidney.ca

**Kids Help Line**
1 (800) 668 6868
www.kidshelp.sympatico.ca

**Lifeline (electronic alert
systems)**
1 (800) 543 3546
www.lifeline.ca

**Lupus Canada**
1 (800) 661 1468
www.lupuscanada.org

**Medical/Physical Aids**
Check with your home care
service, medical supply store
and/or family doctor. Also
some local disease-specific
organizations or Red Cross
branches loan out supplies.

**Social Assistance**
Check Blue government
pages of your telephone
book.

# Important Information

The following is a list of people I can call or visit for help. (Your family doctor, home care case manager or visiting home nurse can help you fill out the information you do not know.)

Your own immediate family not living with you

Family Doctor

Specialists

Home care contact person (they arrange for visiting home nurses, physio and occupational therapy, social workers, respiratory therapists, dietitians, and home care supplies)

Visiting Home Nurses

Homemaking Program

Pharmacist

Volunteer Support Programs

Hospice/Palliative Care Program

Respite Care Program

My Health Care Number and related insurance numbers

# Index

**Yes, I would like to offer my comments to help keep this book up-to-date.**

I am: ☐ a family member ☐ a friend ☐ a neighbor
☐ a professional care provider ☐ a volunteer

Please answer the following questions:

1. What did you like about the content of this book? How did it specifically help you and your family/organization?

2. Are there areas where you would have liked more or less details?

3. Are there areas that were not covered that would help other families/organizations in the future?

Name and telephone number: (optional)

Please mail, fax or e-mail your comments to:

Legacies Inc., 11 Miniot Circle, Scarborough, ON CANADA M1K 2K1
(416) 264-4665, harry@legacies.ca, www.legacies.ca